Oneighty® Devotional

by
Blaine Bartel

Harrison House
Tulsa, Oklahoma

06 05 04 03   10 9 8 7 6 5 4 3 2 1

Oneighty® Devotional
ISBN 1-57794-519-0
Copyright © 2003 by Blaine Bartel
P.O. Box 691923
Tulsa, Oklahoma 74179

Published by Harrison House, Inc.
P.O. Box 35035
Tulsa, Oklahoma 74153

Dedication

This book is dedicated to those people who have made Oneighty® what it is—our students. You've fearlessly shared your faith in Christ, even at the risk of rejection, and you've led the way for a younger generation to follow. I love you all.

—Pastor Blaine

Contents

Got Five?

Let's be honest. We parents and youth leaders want to cram you so full of the Bible that when you burp, revival breaks out. So by now, I'm quite sure your mom, your dad, maybe even your youth leader have given you a shopping cart full of devotional-type manuals and books that would help you become a "radical for God."

You probably got halfway through the first chapter in most of those devotional books and thought, *I'm not trying to be the next Billy Graham here; I just want to be a better Christian.* The good news is that any teenager at any stage of walking with God can make it through these short devotionals. I think you'll find that it will take just five minutes each day.

Here's how it works. We call it the 180 process. **One:** You commit to read and study one Scripture each day. **Eight:** You make a commitment to do the eight weeks in each of the four important areas of your life. **Zero:** You take the zero pledge at the end of each devotional section.

You may be thinking, *Can five minutes a day amount to any kind of real change in my spiritual life?* Fair question. Five minutes a day is probably an improvement on your current spiritual pace. If this simple daily time with God became a habit for life (hint, hint), then at the end of your life (assuming you're about fifteen years old and you'll live to be eighty, give or take a few years on either end) you will have spent the equivalent of eighty complete twenty-four hour days with God.

So take the challenge. **Give five minutes a day to God and watch what happens.** Your life is about to do a 180, moving in new directions that you never dreamed possible. What are you waiting for? Your little brother probably just stole the remote while you were reading this, so turn the page and get started right now. Uh, you do have five minutes, don't you?

Do Eight

ONE: Take the book out wherever you are. Notice the mobility. It's not heavy. Nor is it categorized as big. It's designed for easy transport—a school bag, or a purse perhaps. Your five minutes each day could be anyplace—in a car, in a park, at a bus bench, during your lunch break, in the morning, in the evening, in the locker room after practice…. You get the point.

TWO: Start on day one. (It's becoming crystal clear now.)

THREE: Read the study verse out loud to yourself several times and try to memorize it. Your faith in God will grow and increase the more you hear yourself speaking God's Word. (Romans 10:17 says so—see day one.)

FOUR: Read the devotional.

FIVE: Get ready for the fun to kick in.

SIX: Pray the Commitment Prayer.

SEVEN: If you want a few bonus minutes of reading inspiration, break out your Bible and check out some of the best nonfiction you'll ever read.

EIGHT: Check off day one, put your book in a safe place, take a deep breath and say, "I did it!" Look at your watch. Wow! A great sense of accomplishment in just five minutes!

Oneighty.Truth

The Word of God, found in the Bible, is the manual Jesus has left us to teach us His ways, direct our lives, and give us the power we need each day to serve Him. It is truth, when lived out, that will redefine who you are, where you are going, and what you are able to do. At the completion of the next thirty-one days, the Word of God is going to be more real and alive to you than ever before. Your mind is going to be renewed. You're going to be thinking differently. Yes, you are about to experience a 180-degree turnaround. So go ahead. Why not start with turning the page?

//oneighty.truth

01

01

01 sun
02 mon
03 tue
04 wed
05 thu
06 fri
07 sat

So then faith cometh by hearing, and hearing by the word of God.

ROMANS 10:17

OUT LOUD

Did you know that studies have shown that the human brain actually exists in some WWE wrestling events…and has been proven to retain more than twice the information it receives by both seeing and hearing, as opposed to seeing alone?

Have you ever gone to a live sports event? (Sorry, all you little Hulksters, WWE would not qualify.) Being there live is really cool, but you miss a bunch of the information about the game by not hearing a TV announcer.

Seeing and hearing increase your knowledge. That's why it's important to not just read the Word of God, but to say it out loud. Then you're hearing too, and the Bible promises that your faith will be on the increase.

COMMITMENT PRAYER

Father in heaven, I am bold to pray and speak the Word of God out loud; and I know that as I do, my faith in You grows and gets stronger. From this time forward, my level of faith and trust in You and Your Word is going to increase. In Jesus' name, I pray. Amen.

02

01 sun
02 mon
03 tue
04 wed
05 thu
06 fri
07 sat

For in many things we offend all. If any man offend not in word, the same is a perfect man, and able also to bridle the whole body.

JAMES 3:2

CONTROL

This verse says that by controlling the tongue, we are able to control the desires and impulses of the entire body.

When I was just a kid, I did a lot of horseback riding. This, of course, was before the invention of bicycles. One time, while I was riding the dusty trail, my stupid horse managed to get the bridle out of his stupid mouth and I ended up on the stupid ground. I discovered that my horse didn't love me and didn't want to obey me, as I'd once thought. Instead, it was the bridle that made him obedient.

You live in a body that has fleshly desires and wants to commit stupid sins. The way you will be able to control those desires is by speaking the right words. If you talk about sex all the time, guess what you're going to do really soon?

Your words will guide and direct your life, so weigh each one carefully and let the Word of God be a regular part of your vocabulary.

COMMITMENT PRAYER

Heavenly Father, I ask You to help me take control over my tongue and the words that I speak. I make a commitment to encourage others with my words, and I speak God's words over my life. Thank You that this enables me to keep my body and all its desires under Your control. In Jesus' name, I pray. Amen.

03

01 sun
02 mon
03 tue
04 wed
05 thu
06 fri
07 sat

Let the words of my mouth, and the meditation of my heart, be acceptable in thy sight, O Lord, my strength, and my redeemer.

PSALM 19:14

MEDITATE

This Scripture ties the words of our mouths to the meditations of our hearts. See, whatever we think about is what we're going to be talking about with our rather large mouths. Of course, there are always a few in every crowd who fail to think at all before they talk.

When someone talks about meditation, the image that usually surfaces in our minds is a Chinese-looking guy in a toga, sitting cross-legged, his eyes closed and his fingers in circles, humming in G minor. At least it does in my imagination.

However, to His eternal credit, this is not what God has in mind when He tells us to meditate. He's simply asking us to take a few extra moments in our day to really think about and mull over His Word. When you do, you'll gain new revelation and better understanding about how to make it work in your life.

C'mon—try it.

COMMITMENT PRAYER

Lord, thank You for giving me Your Word to think and meditate on every day. I am confident that both my thoughts and my words will be acceptable and pleasing in Your sight. In Jesus' name, I pray. Amen.

04

01 sun
02 mon
03 tue
04 wed
05 thu
06 fri
07 sat

This book of the law shall not depart out of thy mouth; but thou shalt meditate therein day and night, that thou mayest observe to do according to all that is written therein: for then thou shalt make thy way prosperous, and then thou shalt have good success.

JOSHUA 1:8

BACKSEAT

If you're anything like me, people who commit the heinous sin of "backseat driving" drive you absolutely nuts. The constant commands of "slow down" or "look out" or "you just drove through the neighbor's fence" almost become unbearable. To be honest, when I'm in a car, I have to be in the driver's seat. I want to be in control of my life!

Tragically, there are a lot of Christians who are backseat drivers in their very own lives. They're always complaining about the direction they're currently headed, but they don't have the determination to jump into the driver's seat and take the wheel.

God told Joshua that if he would meditate on and do the Word of God, then he'd be able to make his own way prosperous.

In other words, don't sit back and wait for God to do it all. As you study His Word and pray, He'll give you the ability to steer your life exactly where you need to go, and no man will stand in your way.

COMMITMENT PRAYER

Lord, I believe that You have given me everything I need to live my life to the fullest success. No person can stand between me and Your plans for blessing and prosperity in my life. I meditate and do Your Word daily, and I thank You for good success. In Jesus' name, I pray. Amen.

05

01 sun
02 mon
03 tue
04 wed
05 thu
06 fri
07 sat

But he answered and said, It is written, Man shall not live by bread alone, but by every word that proceedeth out of the mouth of God.

MATTHEW 4:4

HOOVER

A few years back, we challenged all the high schools in our city to show up at our youth ministry, Oneighty®, and see which school could consume the greatest number of hamburgers. At that time our youth group numbered 600, and that night over 1500 students showed up. Before we had the burger competition, we ministered the Word of God, and more than 200 received Christ!

During the burger feast, one young man from one of the local schools brought quite an appetite. Before the night was done he had eaten twenty-six hamburgers! Guess what his name was, "Hoover"! I must say, he was very appropriately named. He sucked down those burgers like they were M&Ms.

Jesus said that we couldn't live by bread (or quarter pounders) alone, that we needed a strong spiritual diet of the Word of God. We need to become spiritual "Hoovers" by developing a hefty appetite for God's Word.

As you continue to work your way through this daily devotional book, your hunger for the things of God will continue to grow!

COMMITMENT PRAYER

Lord, I am hungry to know You more and to fill myself daily with the Word of God. Help me to maintain a discipline of a strong, consistent spiritual diet. In Jesus' name, I pray. Amen.

01 sun
02 mon
03 tue
04 wed
05 thu
06 fri
07 sat

And take the helmet of salvation, and the sword of the Spirit, which is the word of God.

EPHESIANS 6:17

WEAPONS

George Patton, one of the late great American army generals, once said as he spoke to his troops, "Your job is not to die for your country, but to cause others to die for theirs." Whether we realize it or not, as Christians we are in a war. The Bible refers to us as soldiers who must fight many battles through the course of our lives. This is not a time for Christians to go "AWOL" on God. The good news is that we don't have to be afraid of any battle we face. God has given each of us an offensive weapon in our armor. It's called the sword of the Spirit, which is the Word of God.

It's time to stop admiring our sword, polishing our sword—and even carrying it. We've got to use it! When we speak the Word of God boldly in faith, that mighty spiritual weapon cuts through every temptation or spiritual opposition that comes our way.

COMMITMENT PRAYER

Father in heaven, I am not afraid of the trials and battles I am currently facing in my life. I am confident to trust in You and know that Your Word is my weapon in battle. I will not lose! In Jesus' name, I pray. Amen.

07

01 sun
02 mon
03 tue
04 wed
05 thu
06 fri
07 sat

Where there is no vision, the people perish.

PROVERBS 29:18

AMUSEMENT

Have you ever been to a huge amusement park? There are actually many things that aren't really that amusing—long lines to get on the "Stomach Turner," little kids sneaking in line ahead of you…. Anyway, have you noticed that the people at those parks completely forgot about their real world for the hours they were there? A really good park will take you into a fantasy world that suspends your personal reality for at least a few hours. That's why people are running so wild! Every head is on a swivel, looking and searching for the next mind-blowing experience.

Proverbs 29 says that without a vision, people will run wild. God hasn't called us to "amusement park" Christianity. While living for Christ is certainly a great experience, it is meant to have focus and direction towards our assignment to serve God's purpose. If you're not already, find a place to focus and serve in your church, and discover the joy of having vision.

COMMITMENT PRAYER

Heavenly Father, I want to thank You for giving me a vision for my life. I am not going to be given over to a meaningless pursuit of things that ultimately won't satisfy my soul. I believe I have an assignment from heaven, and I will fulfill it. In Jesus' name, I pray. Amen.

08

01 sun
02 mon
03 tue
04 wed
05 thu
06 fri
07 sat

For if any be a hearer of the word, and not a doer, he is like unto a man beholding his natural face in a glass: for he beholdeth himself, and goeth his way, and straightway forgetteth what manner of man he was.

JAMES 1:23,24

MIRROR

Many of today's young people have a distorted view of who they really are. Some have believed the lie that we are little more than monkeys that are "fully loaded" with all the options.

Do you remember going to the fair and walking through the maze of mirrors? Some would make you look like Danny Devito, while others made you look as tall as Shaquille O'Neal. Others just made you look plain weird and twisted.

To get a proper perspective on who we really are, we've got to look into a mirror that will give us an accurate and truthful reflection. That mirror is the Word of God. However, when we walk away from God's mirror, we have to remember what kind of person His Word wants us to be. That means that when we look into God's Word, we've got to take more than a casual glance; we need to look with diligent focus.

COMMITMENT PRAYER

Lord, I thank You for the ability to study Your Word and discover all that You have created me to be and do. I will not lose focus on that calling, but will remember the kind of person You have made me as a Christian. The old person is in the past, and I am a new creation in Jesus Christ. In His name, I pray. Amen.

09

01 sun
02 mon
03 tue
04 wed
05 thu
06 fri
07 sat

Submit yourselves therefore to God. Resist the devil, and he will flee from you.

JAMES 4:7

BARK

The other day when I was driving home from our Oneighty® offices and listening to the news, a story was reported that I could hardly believe. A mail carrier was delivering the mail on one of his routes, and a small, but loudly barking, dog proceeded to run towards him with visions of a leg sandwich. In a flash, this veteran mail guy picked up the dog by the back leg and threw him back into his yard. Of course, the owners of the mutt were in the process of filing a lawsuit: the case of the airborne dog.

I don't condone animal abuse (unless one is trying to hurt me first!), but I do see a parallel here. The devil has a lot of Christians running scared as he barks out his threats of fear and failure. The Word says that when we resist him, he will flee. The word *flee* means "to run in terror."

Why not start to put the devil on the run today!

COMMITMENT PRAYER

Father, Your Word has given me authority over the devil and every power of darkness. I resist fear, failure, and any other attack that Satan would bring my way. In the power of Jesus' name, I command Satan to go. Amen.

10

01 sun
02 mon
03 tue
04 wed
05 thu
06 fri
07 sat

And he said unto them, How is it that ye sought me? wist ye not that I must be about my Father's business?

LUKE 2:49

ALONE

Luke 2 tells the story of Jesus and His family visiting Jerusalem for the Feast of Passover. At the time, He was just a boy, only twelve years old. (He had just gotten His first Game Boy.) Anyway, at the end of the feast, His entire family took off without Him. What's even more amazing is that they traveled an entire day before they noticed He was gone!

There's Jesus running around the big city of Jerusalem by Himself. This was the original *Home Alone* script! When Joseph and Mary finally found Him, He was in the temple asking the teachers about God.

Question: When you have some extra time on your hands, what are you doing with it? Time is like money. You can invest it wisely or squander it. Although you can always find and replace lost money, you will never again have the hour or day that just passed.

So the next time your parents forget you somewhere, take some time to learn more about Jesus. (They'll find you soon enough.)

COMMITMENT PRAYER

Lord, I ask You to forgive me for any time I've wasted in the past few weeks. I commit to spend my time wisely, learning more about You and preparing myself to succeed in this world. I thank You that I am growing in wisdom and favor each day of my life. In Jesus' name, I pray. Amen.

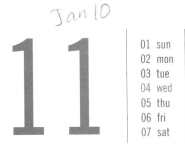

Jan 10

11

01 sun
02 mon
03 tue
04 wed
05 thu
06 fri
07 sat

And be not conformed to this world: but be ye transformed by the renewing of your mind, that ye may prove what is that good, and acceptable, and perfect, will of God.

ROMANS 12:2

UNREASONABLE

There was a great, albeit controversial writer who won the Nobel Prize for literature in 1925. His name was George Bernard Shaw, and he once wrote this: "A reasonable man adapts himself to the world around him. An unreasonable man expects the world to adapt to him. Therefore, all progress is made by unreasonable men."

Mr. Shaw is echoing the Scripture that encourages us to avoid conforming to the world's mold, and to instead be proponents of godly change by thinking His thoughts. I call this unreasonable Christianity.

Reason will tell you to go with the flow. Reason will tell you that if everyone else in your school is doing drugs, then there's nothing wrong with your doing the same. Reason will tell you that if everyone else is losing their virginity, you should too.

It's time to be unreasonable. Changing your thoughts will change your actions. Changing your actions will change the world. So make a change.

COMMITMENT PRAYER

Father, I am determined to live a life of unreasonable Christianity. I am not going to be moved by the tide of this world or my feelings, which may be contrary to what is right according to the Word of God. I reject the world's mold for my life, and I renew my thoughts every day. In Jesus' name, I pray. Amen.

12

Jan11

01 sun
02 mon
03 tue
04 wed
05 thu
06 fri
07 sat

And being fully persuaded that, what he had promised, he was able also to perform.

ROMANS 4:21

PERSUADED

Martin Luther was an Augustinian monk in the 1500s who was shocked by the corruption in the church in his day. The religious hierarchy of his day demanded money and penance from the people who wanted their sins forgiven. According to their traditions, prayers were to be given to God through the mediator of a priest.

Finally, young Luther went to Whittenburg castle and nailed a ninety-five-point thesis of his convictions on a wooden door. The core truth of his conviction was that every believer is justified by personal faith in God, and not by works. He launched the great Reformation and eventually suffered excommunication and public condemnation from the church.

But Martin Luther was fully persuaded that holding fast to the truth of the Word of God was far more important than the acceptance of his peers. Like any great spiritual leader, he didn't just talk about faith; he lived it.

COMMITMENT PRAYER

Father in heaven, I thank You for the promises given to me in Your Word. I choose to believe in You, and I am fully persuaded that You will perform Your Word on my behalf as I trust in You. I am not living for the acceptance and approval of men, but of You, Lord. In Jesus' name, I pray. Amen.

Jan 12

13

01 sun
02 mon
03 tue
04 wed
05 thu
06 fri
07 sat

Therefore whosoever heareth these sayings of mine, and doeth them, I will liken him unto a wise man, which built his house upon a rock.

MATTHEW 7:24

ROCK

Have you happened to notice the escalating peril that exists among our young people in America today? Shootings in our schools, teenage pregnancy and abortion, rampant drug use and crime are all sad reminders of a nation that has lost its moral bearings.

America didn't start out this way. Our forefathers boldly prayed for God's guidance and protection. Our nation's public schools once offered morning prayers and unashamedly posted the Ten Commandments in the classrooms.

As a nation, we had values and commitment to truth that were sure and steady, like a rock. Now we are like shifting sand, with instability and an uncertain future on the horizon. As a young person, you can change this. Benjamin Franklin once stated, "He who shall introduce into public affairs the principles of primitive Christianity will change the face of the world."

Know what you believe, and then make what you believe known!

COMMITMENT PRAYER

Father, I am determined to build my life on the unshakable rock of the Word of God. When storms and trials come, I am not going to be moved away from my faith in You. I pray that my country and its leaders will return to trusting You. In Jesus' name, I pray. Amen.

Jan 13

14

01 sun
02 mon
03 tue
04 wed
05 thu
06 fri
07 sat

While we look not at the things which are seen, but at the things which are not seen: for the things which are seen are temporal; but the things which are not seen are eternal.

2 CORINTHIANS 4:18

RADIO

In October 1982, Wisconsin was playing Michigan State in a college football game at Badger Stadium. There were more than 60,000 Badger fans in attendance watching their beloved Badgers get soundly beaten by the boys of Michigan State. However, at completely random and unusual times during the game, much of the crowd would break out in a loud cheer for no apparent reason! Other fans and players looked on in amazement, wondering why.

They soon discovered that thousands of fans had radios and were tuning in to the World Series game seventy miles away as the Milwaukee Brewers were beating the St. Louis Cardinals. These fans from Milwaukee had found something to cheer about.

There's a lesson to be learned here. When things are going poorly around you, it's time to tune in to a different source. When you plug in to the Word of God and allow the Holy Spirit to inspire you through prayer, victory can be yours even when your circumstances tell you that you're on the losing end.

Keep your focus on the eternal, and the temporal will change.

COMMITMENT PRAYER

Father, I choose to keep my eyes on things that are unseen. My circumstances are all subject to change, and I am trusting in Your Word to bring victory to every area of my life. Thank You for Your faithfulness and Your mercies that are new every morning. In Jesus' name, I pray. Amen.

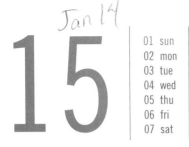

15

Jan 14

01 sun
02 mon
03 tue
04 wed
05 thu
06 fri
07 sat

But now hath he obtained a more excellent ministry, by how much also he is the mediator of a better covenant, which was established upon better promises.

HEBREWS 8:6

WILL

We all know that the Bible is broken up into two parts, the Old and New Testaments. The word *testament* means "covenant" or "will." It simply means a promise.

When people leave this earth, quite often they leave behind a will. A will describes what the benefactors (people who get the stuff) will receive from the remainder of the deceased person's estate.

Since Jesus rose from the dead, I suppose we could call His estate plans a "living will." The New Testament, or will, is an incredible description of all the provision left to us as Christians to carry out our lives successfully while on earth.

Question: If you found out that a certain ultra-rich relative left you in his will, do you think you'd show up for the reading of the will after his passing? Yeah, you'd be there with a tape recorder and a big yellow highlighter to make sure you found out all that was rightfully yours! Jesus left you in His will. He's left you forgiveness, healing, favor, financial prosperity, and a whole lot more. But no one's going to track you down and force it on you. You must read it and put yourself in a position to receive what God already wants you to have.

COMMITMENT PRAYER

Heavenly Father, I am so grateful that You didn't leave me alone or hopeless on this earth. You have promised to provide for every one of my needs. As Your child, I am bold to receive the multiplied blessings that You've promised me in Your Word. And for all that You continue to give me, I will return to You the praise and the glory. In Jesus' name, I pray. Amen.

16

Jan 15

01 sun
02 mon
03 tue
04 wed
05 thu
06 fri
07 sat

The fool hath said in his heart, There is no God. They are corrupt, they have done abominable works, there is none that doeth good.

PSALM 14:1

FOOL

There is no God. All of creation was just one huge cosmic accident. There was no hand of the Almighty that made a trillion or so stars. One day, they just decided to make themselves. And no invisible power keeps each one on a steady course. The earth gave itself day and night and then tilted itself so that we get seasons.

The human heart keeps on pounding for about eighty years without even faltering. A kidney somehow learned how to filter poison from the blood and leave the good stuff alone. I wonder who gave human tongues the flexibility to form words and a cranium to know what they mean, but denied these abilities to the rest of creation. Who showed a womb how to take the love of two people and form a baby with just the right number of fingers, eyes, and ears, and with hair in all the right places, and then decide to bring that baby on into the world when it's ready to sustain itself?

There is no God? Only a fool would make such a lame assumption. And you're no fool!

COMMITMENT PRAYER

Lord, You said that we were fearfully and wonderfully made. The wonder of Your creation daily speaks of Your character and attributes. I thank You today that since You had the ability to create this incredible universe, You can certainly take care of my world. I trust You and am bold to proclaim Your awesome works. In Jesus' name, I pray. Amen.

17

01 sun
02 mon
03 tue
04 wed
05 thu
06 fri
07 sat

I press toward the mark for the prize of the high calling of God in Christ Jesus.

PHILIPPIANS 3:14

PASSION

An old country preacher from Mississippi used to pray this prayer every morning when he got up: "O Lord, give Thy servant this morning the eyes of the eagle and the wisdom of the owl. Illuminate my brow with the sunshine of heaven. Possess my mind with love for people, turpentine my imagination, grease my lips, electrify my brain with the lightning of Your Word. Fill me plumb full of the dynamite of Thy glory. Lord, anoint me all over with the kerosene of salvation, and set me on fire! Amen." This was a preacher with a passion and desire to serve his God.

The apostle Paul was a man like that. He was consumed with God's call and got up every day with one thing on his mind: the desire to press toward God's goal for his life and nothing else. It's not enough just to know what God's plans and goals are for you. Stir yourself up every day by speaking the Word of God over your life and reminding yourself of God's mission for you on this planet!

COMMITMENT PRAYER

Heavenly Father, I thank You that You have purpose and direction for my life every day. I will not allow apathy or carelessness to find its way into my walk with You. Right now, I stir myself up to seek You with a passion and to fulfill Your assignment for my life. In Jesus' name, I pray. Amen.

18

01 sun
02 mon
03 tue
04 wed
05 thu
06 fri
07 sat

Blessed are they which do hunger and thirst after righteousness: for they shall be filled.

MATTHEW 5:6

THIRST

Dogs are loyal animals. But every now and again you come across a dog that is a few milkbones short of a full bag. Years ago we had a dog that would not bark. His name was Buffy. We knew Buffy could bark, because he did once while he was still a puppy, but never again.

One day we went out and put Buffy in the kennel in the garage. We came back late that evening and completely forgot he was still in his small kennel. Something came up, and we had to leave again the next morning and didn't get back to the house for another three days.

All of a sudden, someone said, "Where's Buffy?" My heart sank. All I could picture in my mind was a dead dog who hadn't been able to bark to save itself. I didn't even want to go look. When I finally did, there he was, a complete mess (I'll let you figure out how), jumping around and, of course, silent. When I let him out, I have never seen an animal run so fast to the water dish. That was the thirstiest mutt I have ever seen in my life.

You know what? When you go without spiritual things for a while, rather than getting more and more thirsty, complacency will begin to set in. If you want to stay thirsty for God, drink till you're full of the living water daily. The more you drink, the more you're going to want! And if you ever get locked in a garage, holler!

COMMITMENT PRAYER

Lord, the Bible says that Your Word is the bread of life and the Holy Spirit is the living water. I commit to stay on a steady diet of both, maintaining my hunger and thirst for the things of God. The more of Your Word I know, the more I want to know. Thank You that as I hunger and thirst for righteousness, I am filled and satisfied. In Jesus' name, I pray. Amen.

19

01 sun
02 mon
03 tue
04 wed
05 thu
06 fri
07 sat

All scripture is given by inspiration of God, and is profitable for doctrine, for reproof, for correction, for instruction in righteousness.

2 TIMOTHY 3:16

EVIDENCE

Many innocent people in America have gone to prison for years because of circumstantial evidence against them. From all outward appearances, it looked like they were guilty, and there were no witnesses of the crime to declare their innocence.

We have all had times in our lives when we were unjustly accused of things. There may have been circumstances that made us look guilty, but only we knew the truth.

Our adversary, the devil, tries to bring circumstantial evidence against us all the time. He'll mount some kind of circumstantial case against you, telling you you're depressed or broke or sick or useless.

The good news is that we have a witness that will come to our defense—the Word of the living God! Second Timothy 3:16 says God's Word is profitable for reproof. The Word reproves us for real, not circumstantial, evidence. So when circumstances challenge you that are contrary to the will of God, found in His Word, you must give voice to the witness of God's Word to plead your case and walk away free and delivered!

COMMITMENT PRAYER

Father, I thank You that in every trial of my life, You have given me an Advocate, Your own Son, Jesus Christ. And Jesus has given me Your Word as a witness that testifies against every circumstance in my life that is contrary to Your purpose and will for my life. I stand firm against depression, lack, sickness, and any other destructive force sent my way. Your promises to me are true and sure! In Jesus' name, I pray. Amen.

20

01 sun
02 mon
03 tue
04 wed
05 thu
06 fri
07 sat

Know ye not that they which run in a race run all, but one receiveth the prize? So run, that ye may obtain.

1 CORINTHIANS 9:24

GOLD

The apostle Paul said life is like a race and we can win it or lose it. In this race we are not competing against other people, but against our own potential. Inside all of us God has planted seeds of potential, and our winning or losing depends on what we do with those seeds. We can develop them or neglect them.

Many people try to take shortcuts or even cheat in life to get ahead. They may fool people, but they will never fool God. In 67 A.D. Nero, the emperor of Rome, decided to compete in a chariot race. Right in the middle of the event, he fell off his chariot and never finished the race. The judges, under extreme pressure from the emperor, declared him the winner anyway. The emperor was able to manipulate the judges into overlooking his undeveloped athletic potential.

But in the race of life, we can't fool God. He sees what we do or don't do with our potential.

Purpose in your heart that you will run your race in life to win by developing all the potential you have. Have you been given a musical gift that you are neglecting? Do you have a gift in science or mathematics that you have allowed to be undeveloped?

You may not even know where your potential is. Part of the race is sometimes working to discover what gifts God has put inside us. It takes hard work and practice to discover and develop our potential.

Don't waste any time. Get started today.

COMMITMENT PRAYER

God, please open my eyes to all the potential You have deposited inside me. Give me the passion to pursue Your best and the determination to develop all You have given me. I want to win this race called life. Help me never settle for second best. In Jesus' name, I pray. Amen.

21

01 sun
02 mon
03 tue
04 wed
05 thu
06 fri
07 sat

That ye be not slothful, but followers of them who through faith and patience inherit the promises.

HEBREWS 6:12

WHATEVER

It's not the strongest or most talented who win in life; it's the most persistent.

I like the persistence of Alvin Straight, a seventy-three-year-old farmer who lived in Laurens, Iowa. His eighty-year-old brother, whom he hadn't seen in seven years, had a stroke, and Alvin thought it would be good to visit him. The problem was that his brother lived in Mt. Zion, Washington—240 miles away. Alvin didn't have a driver's license, didn't like public transportation, and didn't want to bother anyone to take him, so he found another way. He hitched a ten-foot trailer to his lawn-mowing tractor and started driving the back roads to see his brother. Alvin didn't have to worry about getting a speeding ticket—he could only travel five miles per hour. It took him six weeks, but he finally got there.

Sometimes in life we may feel as if we are stuck on a tractor going only five miles per hour. But remember the race between the hare and the tortoise. It's not the fastest who win but the most persistent. At times you may not feel as if you are making great progress. Don't quit! As long as you keep your foot on the gas pedal, you will eventually get to your goal—even if you are on a tractor.

COMMITMENT PRAYER

Lord, help me to be focused on the goals You have for me and persistent at reaching toward them. Show me the things that are unimportant, so I can avoid them. And show me the things that will help move me toward your goals. I will be persistent even when I feel as if I'm moving slowly, because I know through Your help I will always be where I need to be, when I need to be there. In the name of Jesus, I pray. Amen!

22

01 sun
02 mon
03 tue
04 wed
05 thu
06 fri
07 sat

But the word of the Lord endureth for ever.
And this is the word which by the gospel
is preached unto you.

1 PETER 1:25

EVERLASTING

Many people throughout history have tried to destroy the written Word of God, the Bible. In the 1930s, Communist leader Joseph Stalin ordered that Russia be purged of all Bibles. This order was carried out with a vengeance.

Years later, after Stalin had died, Russia softened its stand against Bibles and allowed missionaries to distribute them to the people. One missionary team was having difficulty getting Bibles shipped from Moscow to the city of Stavropol. They heard about a warehouse outside the city where thousands of Bibles had been stored, and they asked if they could have them to distribute to the people. The government answered yes. The Bibles in the warehouse turned out to be thousands of the ones Stalin had confiscated in the 1930s. God had supernaturally preserved them so they could later be redistributed to the people. The Bible had survived Stalin's hateful attack and, even when he had died, its message still lived on.

Many people have tried to stamp out God's Word, but they have all failed. God's Word will endure forever. In fact, the Bible is still the number-one selling book of all times. God's Word and its promises are everlasting, and they are waiting for you to take full advantage of them today.

COMMITMENT PRAYER

Lord, thank You for Your written Word, which instructs me, comforts me, and reveals to me Your great promises. May I never take Your Word for granted or neglect to study it daily. Help me to keep Your Word in my heart, that I might not sin against You. In Jesus' name, I pray. Amen.

23

01 sun
02 mon
03 tue
04 wed
05 thu
06 fri
07 sat

Be not deceived; God is not mocked: for whatsoever a man soweth, that shall he also reap.

GALATIANS 6:7

LAW

God has established laws that govern our universe. We all know about the law of gravity. But if I stand on top of a building and say to myself, "I don't believe in this law called gravity," then proceed to jump off the roof, my not believing in the law won't keep me from becoming one with the pavement. The law of gravity works whether or not I like it or believe in it.

There is another law many people don't know about, and that is the law of sowing and reaping. It says that whatever people sow is what they will reap. Laws are created to help benefit us—if we obey them. Now, some laws the government makes don't always make sense, but we do have to obey them.

Listen to these real life laws. It's illegal to spit against the wind in Sault Sainte Marie, Michigan. And goats can't legally wear trousers in Massachusetts. These laws don't make sense, but they are still laws. Fortunately for us, God's laws make perfect sense and are simple. If you want friends, then sow friendship toward others. If you want finances, then give finances to others. Whatever you need or want, just sow that to others and that is what you will reap.

COMMITMENT PRAYER

Lord, thank You that You have established the law of sowing and reaping for my benefit. Help me to take advantage of it by sowing good things, that I may reap good in return. Help me to avoid sowing bad seed, that I may avoid reaping a bad harvest. Thank You for the great harvests that are yet to come in my life. In Jesus' name, I pray. Amen.

24

01 sun
02 mon
03 tue
04 wed
05 thu
06 fri
07 sat

If you wait for perfect conditions, you will never get anything done.

ECCLESIASTES 11:4 TLB

SAFE

We have all heard people tell us to "play it safe" in life. But the ones who experience great success in life are those who take the right risks.

In baseball, Babe Ruth held the record for the most home runs, but he also held the record for the most strikeouts. Why? Because he didn't play it safe. He didn't try for a single or double when he was at bat. When he was swinging, it was for a home run. He swung so hard, one of two things was going to happen. Either he was going to miss, which only meant he could take another try, or he was going to knock the ball out of the park.

When life pitches you the ball, you can play it safe and wait for the perfect pitch, which rarely comes, or you can increase your chances of hitting it out of the park by swinging more and waiting less.

Do you have a dream for a career that seems too big, and are you tempted to shoot for less because you're afraid to fail? Do you want to witness to a friend but fear striking out, so you don't try?

Those who are inducted into life's hall of fame are not the ones who play it safe; they play to win. Swing at your dreams. You just might surprise yourself with a home run. You will never know until you try.

COMMITMENT PRAYER

Lord, help me not to be afraid to take the right risks. I don't want to confuse recklessness with taking risks. But I also don't want to get to the end of my life and wonder what I might have been if I would have taken a few more swings. Give me the needed discernment to know when to swing and the strength to hit the ball out of the park. In Jesus' name, I pray. Amen!

25

01 sun
02 mon
03 tue
04 wed
05 thu
06 fri
07 sat

Christ hath redeemed us from the curse of the law, being made a curse for us: for it is written, Cursed is every one that hangeth on a tree.

GALATIANS 3:13

SUBSTITUTE

One day two brothers were playing fetch with their faithful dog by a river near their house. One of the boys threw the stick, and the excited dog took off like lightning after it. Just before the dog reached the stick, he heard his master scream. The dog turned to see a six-foot diamondback rattlesnake coiled and ready to strike the boy. The snake missed the boy and struck the fearless dog six times. The boy escaped unharmed. Fortunately the dog lived, and he was later inducted into the Texas hall of fame for pets.

Sin, just like that coiled-up, venomous snake, is ready to strike at us. But Jesus stepped between us and sin, taking upon Himself all the punishment that our sins deserved. He died on the cross in order that we might go free. By His sacrifice He has broken the power of sin in our lives. We no longer have to be slaves to any sin. We can walk away from its temptation by the power of Jesus' sacrifice on the cross.

COMMITMENT PRAYER

Lord Jesus, thank You for taking the punishment that my sins deserved. Thank You that by Your sacrifice I am forgiven and free from sin. By the power of Your name and Word, I will resist temptation and overcome. In Jesus' name, I pray. Amen.

26

01 sun
02 mon
03 tue
04 wed
05 thu
06 fri
07 sat

In all thy ways acknowledge him, and he shall direct thy paths.

PROVERBS 3:6

ANYWHERE

How would you like to know about a path in life that could take you anywhere you want to go? "Is there such a road?" you might ask. There sure is, and it isn't that far from where you're standing right now.

This story tells how one man found that road. A man was hiking through a small, relatively unknown village in the mountains of Europe, and he came across an elderly man sitting on his front porch.

"Excuse me, sir! Can you tell me what this village is known for?" the visitor inquired of the old man.

The old man pondered for a moment, then replied, "I don't rightly know, other than it's the starting point to the whole world. You can start here and go anywhere you want."

That is sound advice. The same is true for you. If you are not where you want to be today in your career, finances, relationships, walk with God, or any other area, then you can start where you are today and get to anywhere you want to be. You are standing on the path to anywhere you want to go. Do you want to be a doctor, lawyer, pilot, or maybe a minister? All you have to do is make the decisions that will take you down that path. You can start now, right where you are today.

COMMITMENT PRAYER

Lord, help me to take the steps today that will lead me to where I need to be tomorrow. Show me if I am on a path that I need to change. I don't want to procrastinate with indecision or inaction. Help me to be a person of purpose. In Jesus' name, I pray. Amen.

27

01 sun
02 mon
03 tue
04 wed
05 thu
06 fri
07 sat

Your Master also is in heaven; neither is there respect of persons with him.

EPHESIANS 6:9

RESPECT

One of America's greatest leaders brought needed change to this country as he spoke these enduring words: "I have a dream that my four little children will one day live in a nation where they will not be judged by the color of their skin but by the content of their character." Dr. Martin Luther King Jr. saw the need for racial equality in this world. He saw that it was unbiblical for people to respect a person over another because of the color of their skin.

It is unfortunate that we live in a world where some people do judge others for their skin color, financial status, or social background. Fortunately for us, God doesn't judge us for any of these. He looks at our hearts and not at what's on the outside. God isn't a respecter of persons, and He doesn't love you less or more than He loves anyone else.

Some people feel they have to earn God's love. He can't love you any more than He does right now, because He loves you with all His heart. God may be more pleased with your decisions and actions than another person's, but that doesn't mean God loves them less and you more. People will reap the rewards of the decision to serve or reject God, but that doesn't change God's love for them. God loves the sinner and the saint, the rich and the poor, alike. God is just and fair, and He loves us all the same.

COMMITMENT PRAYER

God, help me to always be just and fair in my relationships with people, just as You are with me. I choose not to judge a person by what's on the outside, but I will look at what is inside. Thank You that You love me with all Your heart and that Your love for me is eternal. Help me to share that love with those around me. In Jesus' name, I pray. Amen.

28

01 sun
02 mon
03 tue
04 wed
05 thu
06 fri
07 sat

Wherefore seeing we also are compassed about with so great a cloud of witnesses, let us lay aside every weight, and the sin which doth so easily beset us, and let us run with patience the race that is set before us.

HEBREWS 12:1

MOTION PICTURE

Tom Landry, Chuck Noll, and Bill Walsh are hall of fame football coaches who accounted for nine of the sixteen Super Bowl victories between 1974 and 1989. What else do they have in common? They also had some of the worst first-season records of all the head coaches in NFL history.

We have all had moments in our lives when we were down. What if someone took a picture of us while we were down and that was all we could be remembered for? Fortunately for us, life isn't made of a single snapshot.

Life is a motion picture. Any good action movie has suspense—that moment when we are on the edge of our seats because it looks as if the hero isn't going to make it. That's what makes the movie exciting. And that's what makes the motion picture of our lives exciting, too.

So if you're down at the moment, don't quit. Get back up on your feet—the camera is still rolling. Don't make a movie about a quitter—make one about a hero who never gives up. All of heaven is watching and cheering you on. You can do it.

COMMITMENT PRAYER

Lord, I choose to make the motion picture that You're filming of my life an action-packed blockbuster. When the enemy attacks, I will resist him, steadfast in the faith. I will counterattack by speaking Your Word. I will not be discouraged when it seems I am down, because through You I can get back up. In Jesus' name, I pray. Amen.

29

01 sun
02 mon
03 tue
04 wed
05 thu
06 fri
07 sat

Now faith is the substance of things hoped for, the evidence of things not seen.

HEBREWS 11:1

UNSEEN

Before the turn of the twentieth century, Bishop Milton Wright used to travel to colleges and speak about the soon second coming of Christ. One evening, while eating supper at a college president's house, Bishop Wright was asked by his host why he was so sure Christ was returning at any moment. He responded, "My good sir, everything that man can accomplish he has already done."

The president of the college politely said, "I respect your opinion, but I disagree. Man hasn't flown yet."

Bishop Wright was taken aback that someone would disagree with him and firmly responded, "If God intended man to fly, He would have made him like the angels and created him with wings."

Bishop Wright limited his world by his ability to believe what he could see. However, he did have two sons who could believe in something even before they could see it. They were Orville and Wilbur Wright. They built and flew the first airplane.

Some people can't believe it if they can't see it, taste it, or touch it. But God asks us to live and walk by faith. We can't always see His promises to us at first, but we are asked to take Him at His Word. When He said, "By Jesus' stripes you were healed," He asked us to believe we are healed even though we may not feel healed. Before we ever see it, we must first believe it. Then we will receive it.

COMMITMENT PRAYER

Lord God, help me not to limit my world by unbelief. I choose to believe that the promises of Your Word are mine even before I see them with my natural eyes. I will walk by faith and not by sight alone. In Jesus' name, I pray. Amen.

30

01 sun
02 mon
03 tue
04 wed
05 thu
06 fri
07 sat

What shall we then say to these things?
If God be for us, who can be against us?

ROMANS 8:31

ROOKIE

Greg Norman, a golf legend, was in a certain tournament where he was having an exceptionally great game. As he teed off one hole he had a perfectly straight and long drive. An excited fan from the crowd yelled out to Greg, "You're the man!"

Greg stepped back and watched as a young rookie on the tour teed up his ball. The young rookie choked under the pressure of playing next to such a seasoned veteran as Greg Norman. He hit a lousy hook that went deep into the rough. Instantly a spectator shouted out some words of encouragement to the young golfer, "You're with the man!"

Sometimes we may feel like that rookie golfer who is having a bad day. At that time we must always remember that heaven is shouting out to us, "It's okay! You're with the Man!" Our God is for us, and it doesn't matter who is against us or what problems come our way. With God on our side, we can't lose. Our victory in life isn't based on our performance anyway; it is based on what God has done for us. All we have to do is remain standing, knowing that we are with the Man.

COMMITMENT PRAYER

Lord, I know that my acceptance by You isn't based on my performance. It is based on my faith in Christ's performance at the cross. I believe that Jesus' sacrifice at the cross has made me complete. Thank You that no matter how I am doing, You never leave me or forsake me. I am grateful that I am with the Man. In Jesus' name, I pray. Amen.

31

01 sun
02 mon
03 tue
04 wed
05 thu
06 fri
07 sat

I have fought a good fight, I have finished my course, I have kept the faith.

2 TIMOTHY 4:7

C.D.

The most unusual fight happened in the early 1900s. A boxer known as C.D. was furiously swinging at his opponent without much success. Fed up with his opponent's ability to avoid his punches, C.D. put all his might into one single punch, hoping that it would knock his challenger's lights out. He swung so hard that when his opponent moved out of harm's way of his punch, C.D. wasn't able to stop the momentum of his swing. His punch came all the way around and landed right in his own face, knocking himself out. The referee gave the ten count, and C.D. lost the fight.

It sounds weird to us that someone could lose by knocking himself out, but it happens all the time—maybe not in a boxing match, but in the arena of the great game called life. We are in a fight called the "fight of faith." The fight has been fixed for us by Jesus' dying on the cross for our sins.

But even though we can't lose in life, many people still do. They either get knocked down by a circumstance, trial, or bad decision of their own and refuse to get back up, or they simply quit the fight and forfeit. You can't lose unless you quit or don't get back up. Don't knock yourself out in a fight you have already won.

COMMITMENT PRAYER

Heavenly Father, thank You that Jesus defeated the enemy by dying on the cross for me. I believe that Jesus has fixed the fight in my favor and that by my faith in His sacrifice for me, I can't lose. It doesn't matter what punches the devil throws at me—I will keep on standing. If I get knocked down, I will get up. If I get tired, I will not quit, because I can do all things through You, who strengthen me. In Jesus' name, I pray. Amen.

32

01 sun
02 mon
03 tue
04 wed
05 thu
06 fri
07 sat

For God hath not given us the spirit of fear; but of power, and of love, and of a sound mind.

2 TIMOTHY 1:7

ODDS

There is a constant battle in all of our lives between the forces of fear and faith. The crazy thing about these forces is that they both really believe something is about to happen. Fear believes the worst is going to happen, while faith believes God's best is already on the way.

Of course, there are many people who put their faith in things that have no promise of return, like buying a lottery ticket. A recent New York City lottery promised the winner 120 million big ones. Lines of people waiting to get tickets went out to the parking lots at convenience stores everywhere. Unfortunately, the odds of winning were one in eighty million.

The Bible tells us that all of God's promises are yes and amen. The power that God gives us to conquer our fears and ignite our faith is His Word. Every promise in the Word of God is your winning ticket.

Hold on tight, and don't let it go!

COMMITMENT PRAYER

Father, I confess with boldness that I have not received a spirit of fear, but I have power, love, and a sound mind. I command all my fears to leave, and I keep my mind stayed on all the promises of God.

Lord, I know You're for me, and no one can be against me. In Jesus' name, Amen.

33

01 sun
02 mon
03 tue
04 wed
05 thu
06 fri
07 sat

Being confident of this very thing, that he which hath begun a good work in you will perform it until the day of Jesus Christ.

PHILIPPIANS 1:6

IDENTITY

Do you remember when the singer "Prince" changed his name to some kind of weird-looking symbol? This is a man who is struggling with a fairly significant identity crisis.

But changing one's name is not completely new. When God told Abram that he was going to give him and his wife, Sarah, a son in their old age, He told Abram to change his name to Abraham. The new name, Abraham, meant "the father of many nations."

In the natural, it was impossible for this couple to bear a child. But God wanted to change their thinking by changing the way they talked, so every time Sarah called her husband, she was saying, "Father of many nations, could you please take out the trash?" Or, "Father of many nations, there's a phone call for you in the back part of the tent."

We can also change our identity by acknowledging the good things God has spoken about us. When we do, we are placing ourselves in a position to receive what He has.

COMMITMENT PRAYER

Lord, I acknowledge all the good things You have given me. Thank You that I'm born again, forgiven of all my sins and growing daily in Your grace and gifts. Because of Your goodness in my life, I am able to share my faith with others more effectively than ever. In Jesus' name I pray. Amen.

34

01 sun
02 mon
03 tue
04 wed
05 thu
06 fri
07 sat

There is a way which seemeth right unto a man, but the end thereof are the ways of death.

PROVERBS 14:12

AGONY

Have you ever watched *Wide World of Sports?* If you have, you no doubt have seen in the opening promo the shot of the skier falling off the side of a huge distance jump, bouncing head-over-heels into a support structure. What you may not know is that he actually meant to do it! Had he gone off the jump at the incredible speed he had amassed on the approach, he would have out-jumped his landing and could have been paralyzed for life, if not killed. Instead, he did something that went against all he had ever learned and ended up with little more than a headache.

There are times in our walks with God when our flesh and minds tell us to do just the opposite of the Word of God. Maybe you've experienced this battle in your tithing or giving at your church. Your mind says you'll have less, but God says you'll have more. Don't do what seems right to you. Obey the Word of God, and avoid disaster!

COMMITMENT PRAYER

Father in heaven, I choose to believe the Word of God over my mind, my body, and my emotions. I am determined not to go the way of the world but to follow closely the principles of the kingdom of God. In Jesus' name I pray. Amen.

35

01 sun
02 mon
03 tue
04 wed
05 thu
06 fri
07 sat

And I heard a loud voice saying in heaven, Now is come salvation, and strength, and the kingdom of our God, and the power of his Christ: for the accuser of our brethren is cast down, which accused them before our God day and night.

REVELATION 12:10

ACCUSER

Do you remember when you were just a little kid and how many times you would threaten to "sue" someone? We live in an age where that is the norm. People are quick to accuse and bring any kind of lawsuit against any person they feel they can get money from. Maybe you remember a few years back when a woman sued McDonald's because her coffee was too hot and she spilled it on *herself!*

That's the way the devil is. He'll accuse you (or God) of things that are not even your fault. Many times, after you've already asked the Lord to forgive you for certain sins, your enemy will come back and try to tell you that you're still guilty. He will accuse you of being insincere or of lacking the "feeling" of being forgiven. Worse yet, he'll accuse God of not keeping His Word, which promises your forgiveness.

Remember that you have an Advocate who represents you and speaks on your behalf. His name is Jesus, and He has given you power over the accuser!

Stand on God's Word, and win your case every time!

COMMITMENT PRAYER

Father, I thank You that You sent Your Son, Jesus, to pay the penalty for my sins and stand as my Advocate. I refuse to listen to the devil and his accusations. I choose to believe what you have said about me in Your Word. In Jesus' name I pray. Amen.

36

01 sun
02 mon
03 tue
04 wed
05 thu
06 fri
07 sat

Now unto him that is able to do exceeding abundantly above all that we ask or think, according to the power that worketh in us.

EPHESIANS 3:20

BEYOND

One older Disney executive recently told the story of how Walt Disney ran his board meetings. Whenever he would present a new idea for one of the Disney theme parks or entertainment programs, he would solicit a response from each of his thirteen board members. If the majority of his board felt his new idea was attainable, he would usually throw it out! Walt Disney wanted to do things that most people thought would be impossible.

As Christians, we know that with God all things are possible. God wants to do above and beyond what we could even begin to think or ask for. And when He gives you a big dream for your life, He will always be faithful to give you a small step each day to fulfill that dream. If we are obedient in each natural step that He gives us, the Lord will take care of the supernatural side of our dreams, which only He can bring to pass.

Don't settle for the average or the mediocre. Go after God's very best for your life!

COMMITMENT PRAYER

Father, I know that I'm capable of thinking and asking for some big things, but You said that You would do even above and beyond my thoughts and requests. I receive everything You have for my life and pursue it with a strong attitude of faith! In Jesus' name I pray. Amen.

37

01 sun
02 mon
03 tue
04 wed
05 thu
06 fri
07 sat

My people are destroyed for
lack of knowledge.

HOSEA 4:6

HMMM

Did you know that most homes valued at more than $250,000 have libraries? That should tell us something. I believe that everything you need for an incredible future and unbelievable success has already been written. And guess what? It's all free! Do you know what it costs to open your Bible? Nothing! How about this: Only 3 percent of all Americans have library cards, and those are free too!

When God says that His people are destroyed for a lack of knowledge, you can begin to see why. You're not lacking opportunity or ability. What you're lacking is the knowledge to uncover your opportunities and the understanding to increase your ability.

Determine to crack open your Bible and other good books that are going to help you reach the goals that God has put in your life.

COMMITMENT PRAYER

Father in heaven, I repent for times in my life when I have not been the student of Your Word that I should be. From this point forward, I am committed to filling my mind with information and knowledge that is going to help me grow and prosper. In Jesus' name I pray. Amen.

38

01 sun
02 mon
03 tue
04 wed
05 thu
06 fri
07 sat

But without faith it is impossible to please him: for he that cometh to God must believe that he is, and that he is a rewarder of them that diligently seek him.

HEBREWS 11:6

BREAKFAST

It has been advertised that Wheaties is the breakfast of champions. Personally, I'd just as soon take Alpha Bits any day of the week.

The truth, however, in the world of sports and life is this: The undisciplined are the breakfast of champions. There is no doubt that those athletes who consistently train and work the hardest come out on top. How many times have we seen championship-caliber athletes or teams lose because of a lack of commitment and discipline?

As a kid, I was a four-time provincial (a province is a version of a state) Judo champion. It did not come easy. I had *good* abilities, but they weren't *great*. However, I was incessantly determined to outwork, outsweat, and outlast every one of my competitors. I beat Japanese guys whose forefathers invented the sport. But even after winning a couple of championships, I was never handed the gold medal for the next competition.

We've got to get up every day to win and be diligent in seeking God and His best for our lives.

COMMITMENT PRAYER

Lord, I refuse to allow a lack of discipline to steal the rewards You have planned for my life each day. I am diligent to pursue You and the promises You have given me in Your Word. I believe that You not only exist, but that You are a good rewarder of those who seek You steadfastly. In Jesus' name I pray. Amen.

39

01 sun
02 mon
03 tue
04 wed
05 thu
06 fri
07 sat

I can do all things through Christ
which strengtheneth me.

PHILIPPIANS 4:13

EXPECTATIONS

Years ago, I heard the story of twin brothers whose father was known in their rather small community as the town drunk. As these two brothers grew up to become men, their lives took two totally different courses. One followed in the footsteps of his father, drinking and partying, eventually becoming an alcoholic. The other son avoided every temptation that had destroyed his father, becoming an upstanding and respected businessman in the community.

When the two brothers were asked why they turned out the way they did, surprisingly they both gave the exact same reply, which was, "What did you expect me to do, growing up with a father like mine?" One son used his father's actions to justify his demise. The other saw his father as an unforgettable motivation to make a better life for himself and his family. One took the attitude of a victim, the other a victor.

When tough times come, choose to be a victor.

COMMITMENT PRAYER

Lord, I thank You by faith that I can do all things through Christ, who strengthens me. I am filled with Your resurrection power, and there is nothing You've given me to do that is impossible. I rely on Your ability and strength each day to overcome every obstacle in the way of Your plans for my life. In Jesus' name I pray. Amen.

40

01 sun
02 mon
03 tue
04 wed
05 thu
06 fri
07 sat

See then that you walk circumspectly,
not as fools, but as wise, redeeming the time,
because the days are evil.

EPHESIANS 5:15,16

CLOCKWORK

USA Today recently published some very interesting facts on how the average American spends time. This is what it said.

In a lifetime, the average American will spend:

- six months sitting at stoplights. (It's better than running them and breaking the law.)
- eight months opening junk mail. (I stopped opening it.)
- one year looking for misplaced objects. (Guilty!)
- two years watching television. (Not in a row!)
- five years waiting in line. (McDonald's drive-through.)
- six years eating. (After you finally get through the drive-through!)

This is what I call the "power of accumulated time" principle. Right now, you can make this principle work *for* you, rather than against you. The best way to stop wasting time is to learn to create schedules for your free time. When you plan out your time and stick with your plan, your productivity in every arena of life will increase *like clockwork.*

COMMITMENT PRAYER

Father, I pray that You will lead me in establishing the right priorities in life. Help me to make the very best of each spare moment of my existence. I want all that I do to be pleasing in Your sight. In Jesus' name I pray. Amen.

41

01 sun
02 mon
03 tue
04 wed
05 thu
06 fri
07 sat

And let us not be weary in well doing: for in due season we shall reap, if we faint not.

GALATIANS 6:9

FINISHER

During the 1968 Mexico City Olympic marathon race, a little-known runner from Tanzania finished in last place, yet ran one of the bravest races ever. Having fallen several times and suffering severe injuries, he was followed by an ambulance and doctors encouraging him to drop out and accept their help and care. He refused and slowly made his way through the streets of Mexico City and eventually back into the Olympic Stadium.

As he literally limped and dragged himself around the final lap of the grueling marathon, the crowd spontaneously rose in applause and cheering. He crossed the finish line and was quickly escorted to the locker room for medical attention.

When reporters asked him the question on everyone's mind, "If you knew you were in last place, why didn't you just quit?" He replied with conviction, "I didn't come 3000 miles to start this race. I came 3000 miles to finish this race."

God is looking for Christian young people who have the heart of a finisher. Every day, we can find reasons to quit and give up. In those moments, we must lift up our eyes to the finish line and stay in the race!

COMMITMENT PRAYER

Father, I will not allow myself to grow weary in my well doing. I am going to reap all of heaven's prizes because I am not going to faint and drop out of my race. I have the heart of a finisher. In Jesus' name I pray. Amen.

42

01 sun
02 mon
03 tue
04 wed
05 thu
06 fri
07 sat

Fight the good fight of faith, lay hold on eternal life, whereunto thou art also called, and hast professed a good profession before many witnesses.

1 TIMOTHY 6:12

ETERNAL

The print ads for one of Nike's very first promotional campaigns showed a runner headed down a two-lane road flanked by a towering forest of Northwest fir trees. The ad said, "There is no finish line." This would eventually become Nike's motto.

The end of our lives on this earth is not the finish. In fact, it is really just the beginning, because in the realm of eternity there is no finish line. It is important for us to take time to judge each choice we make against the backdrop of eternity. Are very many of the things we do going to make any difference in eternity?

The Bible tells us to "lay hold on eternal life" right now. We do this by feeding ourselves spiritually and being prepared to win the souls of people whose eternities still hang in the balance.

We are all in a race. It's a race that we can all win, if we will keep our focus on the everlasting (those things that really count).

COMMITMENT PRAYER

Lord, I have confessed Jesus as my Lord and believe He rose from the dead. Because of that, I thank You that I have the free gift of salvation and eternal life. My focus is not on the temporary, fleeting elements of this earth, but on those things that will endure forever. In Jesus' name I pray. Amen.

43

01 sun
02 mon
03 tue
04 wed
05 thu
06 fri
07 sat

For a just man falleth seven times, and riseth up again: but the wicked shall fall into mischief.

PROVERBS 24:16

NEVER

Winning at life doesn't mean you never get knocked down. It simply means that you get back up.

Some of the most successful people had big failures in their lives. Clint Eastwood was fired from Universal Pictures in 1959 because they said he talked too slowly, but that didn't keep him from acting. Walt Disney went bankrupt seven times in his life, but that didn't keep him from building. Vincent Van Gogh sold only one painting in his lifetime, but that didn't keep him from painting. Henry Ford forgot to put reverse in his first automobile, but that didn't keep him from continuing to build cars.

The Word of God doesn't say you will never fall, but it does say you will never lose—as long as you get back up. In order to become all that God created you to be, you are going to have to do things you have never done before. And when trying new things, you will fall down from time to time—just as you did the first time you learned to ride your bike. But that's okay as long as you get back up, try again, and learn from your mistakes.

Don't be afraid to fall; only be afraid to have never tried.

COMMITMENT PRAYER

Heavenly Father, thank You for Your mercy and forgiveness when I fall. Give me the strength and courage to get back up and try again each time I fall. Help me to learn from my mistakes, that I may avoid repeating them again. In Jesus' name I pray. Amen.

44

01 sun
02 mon
03 tue
04 wed
05 thu
06 fri
07 sat

Lift up your eyes on high, and behold who hath created these things, that bringeth out their host by number: he calleth them all by names by the greatness of his might, for he that is strong in power; not one faileth.

ISAIAH 40:26

BIG

Have you ever wondered just how big God is? No one really knows God's exact shoe size, but it's definitely bigger than any NBA player's.

When you look out into the heavens on a clear night you can see with the naked eye about 2000 to 4000 stars. But there is much more you do not see. Astronomers estimate that there are over 200 billion billion stars. That is one big number! This will give you an idea just how big this number is: If you could count one star every second, 24 hours a day, for 365 days a year, it would take you 32 years to count one billion stars. And to think you would still have 199 billion billion left to count! It takes Oklahoma road crews a month to fix a pothole in the highway, but God created all those stars in a day by just speaking a word.

Next time you feel alone or outnumbered in life, just walk outside and look at the stars. Remember, the same God who created all those stars knows your name, number, and address, and He loves you and is for you. How could you lose with such a big God on your side?

COMMITMENT PRAYER

Thank You, heavenly Father, that I am not alone in this world. I believe You are with me and are on my side. No matter what the enemy throws my way I believe that You are bigger and that by Your Spirit, I can overcome. Thank You for giving me the victory. In Jesus' name I pray. Amen.

45

01 sun
02 mon
03 tue
04 wed
05 thu
06 fri
07 sat

There is no fear in love; but perfect love casteth out fear: because fear hath torment. He that feareth is not made perfect in love.

1 JOHN 4:18

FEAR

When you listen to fear, it will limit what you try, and that will limit what you accomplish. Many people allow fear to rule their lives. Most of what people fear never even comes to pass. In fact, researchers tell us that 60 percent of our fears are totally unwarranted.

Here's an example to help illustrate the stupidity of giving in to fear. When the locomotive was first invented, a group of people tried to have it banned. Their argument was that if humans traveled faster than 30 miles per hour they would suffocate to death. Now, that sounds silly to us today, but they were panic-stricken by the fear of the unknown.

When you give place to fear, it robs you of faith, and that robs you of God's best. When you do have one of those legitimate reasons for concern, even then you don't have to panic. Give your problem to God and trust Him for the answer. He hasn't given you a spirit of fear but of love and faith, and they will overcome anything in the world.

COMMITMENT PRAYER

Lord, thank You that You have not given me a spirit of fear but of love and faith. I choose not to listen to my fears. Instead, I will listen to Your Word. I confront my fear with faith by speaking Your Word. Thank You that it is my faith that overcomes the world and all the problems in it. In Jesus' name I pray. Amen.

46

01 sun
02 mon
03 tue
04 wed
05 thu
06 fri
07 sat

But God hath chosen the foolish things of the world to confound the wise; and God hath chosen the weak things of the world to confound the things which are mighty.

1 CORINTHIANS 1:27

LAUGH

Have others ever made fun of you because you weren't as good as them at something? If so, welcome to the company of great achievers! Most great achievers in life started out against the odds and were considered by the "experts" to have little hope for success.

When Albert Einstein's father asked his school teacher what profession his son should adopt, he was surprised at the answer. The teacher said, "It doesn't matter. He'll never amount to anything."

But that didn't stop Albert Einstein from pursuing his dream, because he had a passion on the inside that was bigger than the critics around him. Albert Einstein had the last laugh.

The world looks at the outside of a person to see if they have what it takes. God does the opposite. He looks at what's on the inside.

The world may be laughing at you and telling you that you don't have what it takes. Don't be moved by their opinion, because it doesn't really matter. Partner with God and allow Him to bring to the outside what is on the inside. Do this, and you too will have the last laugh.

COMMITMENT PRAYER

Lord, I choose not to be moved by the critics around me. Instead, I am moved by Your Word and what You say I can do. Give me the strength to stand and the power to press on. I believe that through You I will have the last laugh. In Jesus' name I pray. Amen.

47

01 sun
02 mon
03 tue
04 wed
05 thu
06 fri
07 sat

Commit thy way unto the Lord; trust also in him; and he shall bring it to pass.

PSALM 37:5

COMMIT

One day a chicken and pig were walking down a road and saw a sign in a diner window that advertised a breakfast special: "Bacon and Eggs, $2.99." "Wow," said the chicken, "they're advertising my eggs. That makes me feel proud."

The pig wasn't as excited. "Feel the way you want," he snapped. "Your part is only a contribution. Mine is a commitment."

Most people in life only want to make a contribution because a commitment costs much more. God doesn't want a contribution but a commitment to Him.

But God isn't asking anything from us He hasn't done already. God has totally committed Himself to seeing you succeed in life. He didn't send Jesus to earth to make a contribution of a few nice sermons. He sent Him to make a total commitment to us by dying on the cross. He willingly laid down His life to be a sacrifice for our sins. Now, that is commitment.

Are you making contributions to God by giving as little as possible of your time, talents, and money to Him? Or are you totally committed to Him by giving Him your best?

COMMITMENT PRAYER

Lord, thank You for Your unbreakable commitment to me. Even when I have been unfaithful, You have always been faithful. From this day forward, I choose to make a commitment to You. I want to give You my best, not my second best. In Jesus' name I pray. Amen.

48

01 sun
02 mon
03 tue
04 wed
05 thu
06 fri
07 sat

For I know the thoughts that I think toward you, saith the Lord, thoughts of peace, and not of evil, to give you an expected end.

JEREMIAH 29:11

OUTCOME

It doesn't matter where you start in life; it only matters where you finish. You may have been off to a rough start because of bad decisions or events beyond your control. That isn't as important as what you do about it. Most successful people had great obstacles to overcome in the beginning of their lives. Those challenges can actually feed your passion for success.

Michael Jordan failed to make the cut for his high school sophomore basketball team. That's a bad start for someone who wants to pursue a career in the NBA. But Mike did not let that stop him. He decided that, rather than feeling sorry for himself and moping around the house all day, he was going to prove the critics wrong. He said to himself, "I'm going to show the world that I can be a great basketball player." Then he went out and did something about it (it's called practice), and he changed his future. And we all know the rest of the story.

If you are off to a rough start in life it's not that big of a deal, because you still have today to change your tomorrow. You too can achieve your dream through hard work and lots of practice.

COMMITMENT PRAYER

Lord, thank You that it isn't where I start in life that matters, but it's where I end up. I have had some setbacks along the way, but I will not allow them to keep me from my dreams. Thank You that through Christ Jesus, who strengthens me, I can do all things. In Jesus' name I pray. Amen.

49

01 sun
02 mon
03 tue
04 wed
05 thu
06 fri
07 sat

And if children, then heirs; heirs of God, and joint-heirs with Christ; if so be that we suffer with him, that we may be also glorified together.

ROMANS 8:17

MESSAGE

A man was walking along the beach in San Francisco and discovered a bottle with a note in it. To his surprise it read, "To avoid any confusion, I leave my entire estate to the one who finds this bottle." The finder of the bottle was curious and hopeful enough to find out if the note was real. It was. The man inherited six million dollars up front and $80,000 a year thereafter.

Now, don't stop reading this to look for bottles with notes in them. Your name is already in a will that is worth far more than a measly six million dollars. You are in God's will, and He is so wealthy that He uses gold like asphalt, to pave His streets in heaven.

The Bible is God's will. You've probably seen that the Bible is divided into the "Old Testament" and the "New Testament." Before someone passes away they make a "last will and testament" to let people know what they want to happen to their belongings. God gave us His last will and testament in His Word. Every time you open it, you see all the great things that God has given you—things like prosperity, healing, favor, wisdom, peace and victory.

But a will doesn't go into effect until the author passes away. Jesus died on the cross for us, so that we can receive our inheritance now. You don't have to wait to get to heaven to enjoy it; you can start having it today. Open up the Bible and start looking for the good things God has in store for you.

COMMITMENT PRAYER

Heavenly Father, thank You for placing me in Your will. Thank You that anything I will ever need in life is found in Your will. I purpose to read Your Word daily to discover all the good things You want me to enjoy in life. Thank You for all Your wonderful blessings that are mine because of Jesus' sacrifice for me. In Jesus' name I pray. Amen.

50

01 sun
02 mon
03 tue
04 wed
05 thu
06 fri
07 sat

And he said, Who told thee that thou wast naked? Hast thou eaten of the tree, whereof I commanded thee that thou shouldest not eat? And the man said, The woman whom thou gavest to be with me, she gave me of the tree, and I did eat.

GENESIS 3:11,12

RESPONSIBILITY

After Adam and Eve ate the forbidden fruit, God gave Adam a chance to tell the truth and repent. But, instead, Adam did what most people do—he shifted the blame to someone else. The between-the-lines part to his answer was "Hey, God, don't try to pin this on me. I'm the victim here. After all, the woman made me do it. And by the way, weren't You the one who gave me that woman anyway?"

Adam should have taken responsibility for his sin by saying, "It was my fault. I ate the fruit. I did it. I'm sorry." But he took the easy way out and blamed it on others.

You can see how people aren't willing to take responsibility for their actions by this story. One man was sentenced to serve twenty-three years for grand larceny. He sued. The unusual thing about his lawsuit was that he was suing himself for violating his religious beliefs of breaking the law and getting arrested. He asked that the state award him 5 million dollars to support his family while he was in prison. The case was thrown out of court.

People with this kind of attitude never get ahead in life. If you make a mistake, be mature enough to say, "It was my fault, and I'm willing to face the consequences of my wrong decision." Then face it head-on, learn from your mistake, and don't repeat it.

COMMITMENT PRAYER

Lord, help me to take responsibility for my sins and mistakes. I don't want to get caught in the cycle of blaming others for my mistakes. They may have influenced my wrong decisions, but I have the power to make my own choices. Help me to be wise enough to make the right decisions and mature enough to admit it when I make the wrong ones. In Jesus' name I pray. Amen.

51

01 sun
02 mon
03 tue
04 wed
05 thu
06 fri
07 sat

Not slothful in business; fervent in spirit; serving the Lord.

ROMANS 12:11

HUNGER

A family in England received what they thought was a Christmas gift package from some relatives in Australia. The package consisted of what looked to be cooking herbs. They proceeded to stir the herbs into their traditional Christmas pudding. They ate half that evening and placed the remainder in the refrigerator for later. Soon after that they received a phone call from their auntie saying that their Uncle Eric had died and asking if they had received his ashes for burial yet. You can imagine the horror they experienced—not to mention their upset stomachs.

This rather crude, but true story illustrates that we have to be careful what we eat. You've heard it said that you are what you eat. This is true with our spiritual diets as well. If we allow ourselves to eat too much entertainment, we will get spiritually out of shape. Some entertainment is okay, but you want to make sure that isn't the only thing you're feeding your mind and spirit. We must have a well-balanced spiritual diet that consists of feeding our spirits the Word of God.

COMMITMENT PRAYER

God, help me to have a well-balanced spiritual diet. Give me the discernment to avoid entertainment, relationships, or music that would be unhealthy for my spiritual growth. I decide to feed my spirit the Word of God every day. Help me to keep this commitment. In Jesus' name I pray. Amen.

52

01 sun
02 mon
03 tue
04 wed
05 thu
06 fri
07 sat

As a dog returneth to his vomit,
so a fool returneth to his folly.

PROVERBS 26:11

SURF

In 1983, a killer storm rocked the Pacific coastline. A surfer in San Diego carelessly put his life at risk to catch a few good waves. Due to the ferocity of the storm, this young man lost control of his board and suffered serious head injuries. A lifeguard risked his own life to rescue the foolish surfer by dragging his body from the surf to the bottom of a steep cliff. Firemen then risked their lives to lift him up by a rescue line.

Two months later the same surfer was wading his way out into another dangerous surf, when a lifeguard tried to stop him. The rebellious young man ignored the lifeguard's orders to stop and return to shore. The same lifeguard who had saved his life a few months earlier had to place him under arrest this time to keep him from surfing in the dangerous storm.

Some people just don't learn. God's Word tells us that when we sin God forgives us. But that isn't an excuse to keep returning to that sin. Some people feel that they have to catch those few good waves that sin offers. But little do they realize they are putting their life at great risk. Sin's only purpose is to kill, steal, and destroy from your life. God wants you to have abundant life. So when you do make a mistake, ask for forgiveness. Learn from your mistake and avoid making the same one at all costs and enjoy the truly abundant life.

COMMITMENT PRAYER

Lord, please forgive me for my sins. Thank You for cleansing me and forgiving me. I don't want to use Your mercy as a license to keep on sinning. Give me the wisdom and strength to avoid sin. Thank You that I have the power in Jesus' name to overcome it. In Jesus' name I pray. Amen.

53

01 sun
02 mon
03 tue
04 wed
05 thu
06 fri
07 sat

Therefore I say unto you, What things soever ye desire, when ye pray, believe that ye receive them, and ye shall have them.

MARK 11:24

BELIEVE

George Washington was a man who believed the Word of God. He wrote to his son in a letter, "Remember that God is our only sure trust."

Washington wrote that from experience and not blind faith. After one battle during the French and Indian War, Washington removed his coat and found four bullet holes in it. The Indian chief who led that attack said years later, "Washington was never born to be killed by a bullet! I had seventeen fair fires at him with my rifle, and after all could not bring him to the ground."

God isn't a respecter of persons. All His promises are for you, too. Unfortunately, many Christians fail to receive all the great things God has in store for them—not because God has withheld them, but because they didn't reach out and receive them through faith.

Is there an area of your life that is falling short of God's best? If so, begin reading passages of Scripture that will build your faith in that area. Then ask God for what you need, and believe you receive it by faith. Then thank Him for it. You may not see an answer instantly, but you know that you have it by faith. So when you are reminded about that need, keep thanking Him for it because it is yours and it's on the way.

COMMITMENT PRAYER

Heavenly Father, thank You that all Your promises are for me today. I believe that when I pray You hear me and that I have the answer to my prayers. What You do for others You will do for me because You are no respecter of persons. In Jesus' name I pray. Amen.

54

01 sun
02 mon
03 tue
04 wed
05 thu
06 fri
07 sat

And these things write we unto you,
that your joy may be full.

1 JOHN 1:4

LETTERS

People often have different views of what love is. Nine-year-old Roger was asked what he thought falling in love was like and commented, "Like an avalanche where you have to run for your life."

Jan, who was also nine, was asked why two people fall in love, and she said, "No one is sure why it happens, but I heard it has something to do with how you smell. That's why perfume and deodorant are so popular."

"I think you're supposed to get hit with an arrow or something, but the rest of it isn't supposed to be so painful," was six-year-old Harlen's response.

These answers seem a little silly, but everyone probably has a little bit different concept of love. The Bible is the best picture of what true love is. Every page is filled with all kinds of different illustrations to help you see just how much you mean to God. It is His personal love letter to you. God inspired every verse to show His unfailing love towards us.

As you take time daily to read God's Word, you will understand and know what true love is.

COMMITMENT PRAYER

Lord, thank You that You love me with selfless love. Help me to understand just how much You love me as I read Your Word daily. Open up my understanding to comprehend just how wide, high, and deep is Your love for me. In Jesus' name I pray. Amen.

55

01 sun
02 mon
03 tue
04 wed
05 thu
06 fri
07 sat

And Saul said to David, Thou art not able to go against this Philistine to fight with him: for thou art but a youth, and he a man of war from his youth.

1 SAMUEL 17:33

CRITICS

There will always be someone who will be glad to tell you why you can't succeed, if you are willing to listen. The world is full of critical people who have failed and want to keep others down with them. Even the most successful people in life have been told by critics why they can't achieve their dreams. When the movie *Star Wars* was first released in 1977, a movie critic gave this negative review: "O' dull new world! It is all as exciting as last year's weather report…." Little did that critic realize the huge success *Star Wars* would have.

If you have critics in your life telling you why you can't succeed, don't listen to them. The good news is that God's opinion of you is the one that really counts. And God is your biggest fan; He believes in you. Every time you read your Bible, you will see God encouraging you and cheering you on. Even when you fall down, He is there to pick you back up. Feed your dreams the encouragement they need by reading God's Word.

COMMITMENT PRAYER

Heavenly Father, I refuse to listen to the critics who tell me all the reasons I can't achieve my dreams. I thank You that You believe in me even when others don't. Thank You that even when I fall, You pick me up and cheer me on. Thank You for the encouragement I find every day in Your Word. In Jesus' name, Amen.

56

01 sun
02 mon
03 tue
04 wed
05 thu
06 fri
07 sat

Fight the good fight of faith, lay hold on eternal life, whereunto thou art also called, and hast professed a good profession before many witnesses.

1 TIMOTHY 6:12

PRIZE

On July 4, 1776, over fifty signers of the Declaration of Independence took a stand against the tyranny of England. If need be, they were even willing to sacrifice their lives on the battlefield and give up their fortunes to protect our country.

The Declaration of Independence was ratified with the blood of brave souls who fought to preserve our freedom. Since then we have had many wars in which soldiers have sacrificed their lives, that this country might remain free.

These heroes have purchased our freedom for us, but we must contend against others who would try to take it from us. Likewise, Jesus has purchased for us spiritual freedom from sin and Satan by dying on the cross for us, but we do have to contend to keep our freedom.

We keep our freedom by resisting Satan's attacks by speaking God's Word. When the devil tries to take something from you that is rightfully yours, find Scriptures that pertain to that area and speak them.

We resist the enemy with the spoken Word of God. When we speak the Word, it reminds Satan that Jesus defeated him and that we are giving him no place in our lives.

Next time you're attacked with sickness, financial lack, or a temptation, speak the Word of God and keep your freedom.

COMMITMENT PRAYER

Thank You, Lord, that You have purchased freedom for me. My freedom didn't come at a cheap price. It cost the life of Your Son, and for that I am so grateful. Since You have set me free, I choose to remain free from sin by submitting myself to You. When the enemy attacks, I will resist him by speaking Your Word. In Jesus' name I pray. Amen.

Make the Zero Pledge

Lord, right now, I make this solemn pledge before You. Zero gray. From this point forward I will see things in black and white, right and wrong. I choose right; I choose the truth. God's Word is the compass that will direct each area of my life from now on. In Jesus' name. Amen.

Oneighty.Friend

The Word teaches us that those who walk with the wise will become wise, but the companion of fools will be destroyed. We cannot overestimate the importance of choosing the right friends. The friends we hang out with every day will have an immeasurable impact on our success and future.

In the next thirty-one days of Oneighty® devotionals, you will discover how to build strong, loyal, and lasting friendships. Go ahead. Turn the page, and let's get started.

//oneighty.friend

02

01

01 sun
02 mon
03 tue
04 wed
05 thu
06 fri
07 sat

He who walks with wise men will be wise, but the companion of fools will be destroyed.

PROVERBS 13:20

STEALING CONTESTS

I was twelve years old and had never stolen anything from a store in my life. I had grown up in church and had always been taught to be honest.

Then along came Scott, and I became his friend. One day we walked out of the local mall, and he began to pull out all kinds of stuff: candy bars, sports cards, hockey tape—even a small alarm clock. He had taken stuff he didn't even need!

I told him I would never steal anything. But I kept hanging out with him every day. One month later we were having stealing competitions to see who could steal the most loot. The police caught up with us a few weeks later. And my parents…

Never mind! I'm starting to have bad flashbacks!

Needless to say, I stopped hanging out with Scott, and the stealing stopped too.

Don't allow any person to steal any virtue in your life.

COMMITMENT PRAYER

Heavenly Father, I am bold to pray the Word of God out loud. I pray that You will give me wisdom to choose the right friends and influences in my life, in Jesus' name. Amen.

02

01 sun
02 mon
03 tue
04 wed
05 thu
06 fri
07 sat

A man who has friends must himself be friendly....

PROVERBS 18:24

NO ONE LIKES ME

I'll never forget the very first youth group I pastored. There was this girl who was always so sad and depressed. She would just stand in the corner of the room by herself before and after each meeting.

One night she came up to me and said, "Pastor Blaine, nobody in this youth group likes me. They're not very friendly!"

She had absolutely never made any attempt to talk to anyone. She always looked so mean and depressed that most were afraid to even approach her. I told her that she—not everyone else—was the problem.

Put a smile on your face. Introduce yourself. Take an interest in others. Friends will follow.

COMMITMENT PRAYER

Father, I commit to be a good friend, and I know that You will send me good friends as a result. Help me to let Your love come out, in Jesus' name. Amen.

03

01 sun
02 mon
03 tue
04 wed
05 thu
06 fri
07 sat

And do not be conformed to this world, but be transformed by the renewing of your mind....

ROMANS 12:2

STICK WITH IT

Did you ever hear of the Kamikaze pilot who flew twenty-one missions? Obviously, he wasn't committed the first twenty times.

The world's standards for relationships are much different from God's. We must make a commitment to follow God's commands about relationships, as found in His Word. And once we make a commitment to the right things, we've got to stick with it until the end.

Anyone can give in to the world's standards. But it takes courage and character to stand up and be different.

COMMITMENT PRAYER

Father, give me strength every day to be transformed and changed by Your Word. Help me to not allow my thoughts and desires to be influenced by an ungodly world. In Jesus' name, I pray. Amen.

04

01 sun
02 mon
03 tue
04 wed
05 thu
06 fri
07 sat

What is desired in a man is kindness, and a poor man is better than a liar.

PROVERBS 19:22

DESIRABLE PEOPLE

We once had a really odd-looking young man in our youth group. He was a happy, outgoing, friendly young man and had girls constantly vying for his attention. All the other guys who thought they were better looking than him couldn't figure it out.

The world says looks, image, and beauty are the highest priorities in relating to one another; but in truth good character and the fruit of the Spirit are what will make you attractive to others. Kindness is what makes you desirable to be around.

COMMITMENT PRAYER

Heavenly Father, help me to work on my inner beauty as much as or more than I work on the outside. Thank You that Your kindness and love are my most important qualities, in Jesus' name. Amen.

05

01 sun
02 mon
03 tue
04 wed
05 thu
06 fri
07 sat

"Have I not commanded you? Be strong and of good courage; do not be afraid, nor be dismayed, for the Lord your God is with you wherever you go."

JOSHUA 1:9

LEAD ON

My pastor, Willie George, asked our church and ministry staff members a powerful question at a recent staff meeting: "Do you want to be popular, or do you want to be a leader?"

Many times when we show courage and strength in our decisions and actions, we will actually lose people we thought were our friends.

God told Joshua not to follow the crowd but to follow his convictions. And God promised to be with him and give him his inheritance. God will do the same for you.

COMMITMENT PRAYER

Father, I believe You have called me to stand out from the crowd. Thank You for giving me strength and courage to never pursue popularity at the expense of righteousness, in Jesus' name. Amen.

06

01 sun
02 mon
03 tue
04 wed
05 thu
06 fri
07 sat

Faithful are the wounds of a friend, but the kisses of an enemy are deceitful.

PROVERBS 27:6

ZIP IT

One of the most embarrassing moments of my life came one Sunday morning when I was guest preaching at a church. I kept noticing the pastor making unusual motions to me from his seat in the front row. I continued to preach, and he continued to motion more and more dramatically. I figured something was wrong, but I didn't know what—until I looked down. There it was, wide open—the dreaded unzipped pants zipper.

"Every head bowed. Every eye closed," I said to the congregation. And up went the zipper.

A true friend will tell you when you've made a mistake, even if it is a little humbling for the moment. And true friendship always has give and take. Learn to accept your role in both.

COMMITMENT PRAYER

Father, thank You for giving me the strength to speak the truth in love to my friends and to accept correction when I need it. Your grace will always be sufficient for both. In Jesus' name, I pray. Amen.

07

01 sun
02 mon
03 tue
04 wed
05 thu
06 fri
07 sat

[Love] bears all things, believes all things, hopes all things, endures all things.

1 CORINTHIANS 13:7

LOOKING BEYOND

At fifteen years old, I determined to be an atheist. I grew up in a dead church and had never seen genuine Christianity.

Yet even when I denied all that God had done and sacrificed for me, He never gave up on me. His people didn't give up on me either. At sixteen years old, my friend and classmate Stu was instrumental in leading me to Christ.

While our closest friends should be those who have strong character and commitment to Christ, we should not ignore others who need God's help. Even when things look bleak in their lives, God's love in us believes, hopes, and endures all challenges to see them reached for Christ.

What person has God been leading you to reach?

COMMITMENT PRAYER

Father, thank You for giving me the courage and boldness to share Your love with others. Help me to never give up on others, no matter how far down they may get. Your love can always bring us through, in Jesus' name. Amen.

08

01 sun
02 mon
03 tue
04 wed
05 thu
06 fri
07 sat

Love never fails. But whether there are prophecies, they will fail; whether there are tongues, they will cease; whether there is knowledge, it will vanish away.

1 CORINTHIANS 13:8

IF YOU CAN

Think about this.

If you can...

- always be cheerful, ignoring your own pains...
- resist complaining about all your troubles...
- eat the same food every day and be grateful...
- understand why people are too busy for you at times...
- overlook offenses committed against you...
- take criticism and blame without resentment...
- treat the rich and poor the same...
- face the world without lies and deceit...
- honestly say that you have no prejudice...

...then you are almost as good as your dog.

They say that a dog is a man's best friend. Why? It's because a dog's love for his master never fails.

COMMITMENT PRAYER

Heavenly Father, Your love is inside me because my heart has been made new. Thank You that Your love in me does not fail, but gives me the ability to be a true friend, in Jesus' name. Amen.

09

01 sun
02 mon
03 tue
04 wed
05 thu
06 fri
07 sat

"Give, and it will be given to you: good measure, pressed down, shaken together, and running over will be put into your bosom. For with the same measure that you use, it will be measured back to you."

LUKE 6:38

LOVE NOW

A wealthy man asked his friend, "Why are people upset with me for being thrifty? You all should know that I'll leave everything to charity when I die."

The friend said, "Let me tell you about the pig and the cow.

"The pig complained about how unpopular he was and said to the cow, 'People always talk about your goodness. Sure, you give milk and cream, but I do better than that. I give bacon and ham! They even pickle my feet! Still, nobody appreciates me. Why not?'

"The cow thought briefly and said, 'Perhaps it's because I give while I'm still living.'"

Learn a lesson from the cow, and give while you still have the opportunity.

COMMITMENT PRAYER

Father, I will not procrastinate to love and to give. I believe as I give that it is given back to me in an even greater measure, in Jesus' name. Amen.

10

01 sun
02 mon
03 tue
04 wed
05 thu
06 fri
07 sat

For God so loved the world that He gave His only begotten Son, that whoever believes in Him should not perish but have everlasting life.

JOHN 3:16

THE GREATEST

This Scripture contains the greatest of all things we could want or give in our lives:

- **God**—the greatest love
- **so loved**—the greatest degree
- **the world**—the greatest expanse
- **that He gave**—the greatest single act
- **His only begotten Son**—the greatest gift
- **that whoever**—the greatest opportunity
- **believes**—the greatest simplicity
- **in Him**—the greatest attraction
- **should not perish**—the greatest promise
- **but**—the greatest difference
- **have**—the greatest certainty
- **everlasting life**—the greatest possession

In this verse, we see the extent of God's friendship toward us. What's amazing is that if you have received Christ, then this same love has been put inside of you!

COMMITMENT PRAYER

Father, You are the greatest friend I could ever have. I thank You for loving me when I wasn't even thinking about You. In Jesus' name, I pray. Amen.

11

01 sun
02 mon
03 tue
04 wed
05 thu
06 fri
07 sat

If anyone among you thinks he is religious, and does not bridle his tongue but deceives his own heart, this one's religion is useless.

JAMES 1:26

TONGUE BUILDER

I was an expert at the art of the cut-down. Even after my conversion to Christ, I used my tongue for the sake of humor to cut down even my closest friends. This was a common occurrence, until one day a girl whose opinion I respected asked to have a private word with me. She rebuked me! I was in shock as she told me how my words had hurt others and would eventually destroy my friendships.

I swallowed my pride and agreed to repent, and those friendships have lasted my entire life.

Realize that the words you speak to others will either build or destroy their lives. Use your tongue to speak words that build!

COMMITMENT PRAYER

Father, I put a watch on my words. I determine to build the esteem and lives of those around me each day, in Jesus' name. Amen.

12

01 sun
02 mon
03 tue
04 wed
05 thu
06 fri
07 sat

Greater love has no one than this, than to lay down one's life for his friends.

JOHN 15:13

SACRIFICE

I remember smuggling Bibles into Communist Russia in 1980. I was just barely out of high school and was so excited to watch God begin to use me to reach people who had never heard about Jesus.

I used to think about how awesome it would be to be a martyr for the cause of Christ. As I grew older, I began to see that we can lay down our lives each day in many other ways. It may be giving up money to help friends go to the mission field. It may be giving personal time to serve in weekly campus ministries. Each day we can lay down parts of our lives for friends who need us and to advance the kingdom of God.

COMMITMENT PRAYER

Father, I commit to lay down areas of my life for my friends and for the kingdom of God. As I do I know You will always meet all of my needs, in Jesus' name. Amen.

13

01 sun
02 mon
03 tue
04 wed
05 thu
06 fri
07 sat

And have no fellowship with the unfruitful works of darkness, but rather expose them.

EPHESIANS 5:11

SHINE

When I was a kid, my most painful moments came when I had to get up in the night to go to the bathroom. Almost without exception, as I walked through the darkness I would stub my toe on one of my brother's trucks or toys. I finally learned my lesson: *Don't walk in the dark!*

We need to shine the light of God's Word on every work of darkness that would try to trip us up. Don't compromise in the dark when you can walk in victory in the light!

COMMITMENT PRAYER

Heavenly Father, thank You that Your Word is a lamp to my feet and a light to my path. I will not be tripped up by any of Satan's traps, in Jesus' name. Amen.

14

01 sun
02 mon
03 tue
04 wed
05 thu
06 fri
07 sat

Let no corrupt word proceed out of your mouth,
but what is good for necessary edification,
that it may impart grace to the hearers.

EPHESIANS 4:29

BABY STUFF

I'll never forget one of my first encounters with somebody else's baby. They told me he was "cute, sweet, and oh-so-innocent." Sure. Then I was made to hold the little thing while he proceeded to throw up green-pea baby food and half-digested milk all over my new shirt! The next baby I would hold would be my own. I no longer trust someone else's offspring!

When we allow corrupt, profane, and cutting language to become a part of our vocabulary, we are no different than that baby—except that we choose to do it even though we know better. Treat your friends and family to a vocabulary void of verbal vomit: Let each word be seasoned with life and hope.

COMMITMENT PRAYER

Father, thank You for giving me the power to control my tongue and use my words to impart grace and edification to all who hear me. In Jesus' name, I pray. Amen.

15

01 sun
02 mon
03 tue
04 wed
05 thu
06 fri
07 sat

Brethren, if a man is overtaken in any trespass, you who are spiritual restore such a one in a spirit of gentleness, considering yourself lest you also be tempted.

GALATIANS 6:1

LIFELINE

My brother in Christ and one of my closest friends had lost his step. He had come out of the terrible world of drug abuse and been completely delivered. Through a series of bad decisions, though, he had eventually found himself right back in that dangerous world. He needed somebody.

No one sat back and pointed fingers. My pastor, many of his other friends, and I reached out to him with the love of God. Sin forced him to pay a heavy price in his personal life, but thankfully he was restored in his relationship with God.

As believers, we have a responsibility to reach out and throw a lifeline when our friends are in spiritually dangerous waters. It's up to them to decide whether to take it, but we must at least care enough to give them a chance.

COMMITMENT PRAYER

Father, help me to find those sheep that have gone astray from the flock. Show me how to pull them back in, in Jesus' name. Amen.

16

01 sun
02 mon
03 tue
04 wed
05 thu
06 fri
07 sat

"And whenever you stand praying, if you have anything against anyone, forgive him, that your Father in heaven may also forgive you your trespasses."

MARK 11:25

FORGIVE

One day, if you haven't already, you will go out and get yourself a job. Why? Is it because you see a restaurant like McDonald's and want to use your spare time to help them sell a bunch more hamburgers? Of course that's not why. You have a plan to make yourself some money!

Many people have the wrong idea about forgiveness. They think if they forgive, they're just helping someone else. But forgiveness is not just for the other person's good; it's for your own good. When you forgive someone, you are making a statement: *No person's offense can ever stand between God's blessing and me.*

Unforgiveness says a person is bigger than God's ability in your life. So forgive others quickly. It's for your own good.

COMMITMENT PRAYER

Father, in Jesus' name, I make a choice today to truly forgive any person who has wronged me. Lord, You are able to cause me to overcome anything anyone does to hurt me. In Jesus' name, I pray. Amen.

17

01 sun
02 mon
03 tue
04 wed
05 thu
06 fri
07 sat

Death and life are in the power of the tongue, and those who love it will eat its fruit.

PROVERBS 18:21

ELEVATE

When I was nineteen years old a good friend said one sentence to me that changed my life: "I believe you will be a strong leader in the body of Christ."

Honestly, I had never thought of myself as a leader of any kind, never mind a "strong leader." But from that moment on, I began to see myself stepping up to this new ideal for my future. Since that day, God has enabled and blessed me with the grace to lead thousands in kingdom advancements.

Your words have that kind of power. Your words can either lift people to new levels of accomplishment, or destroy them. Choose them well.

COMMITMENT PRAYER

Father in heaven, my words are meant to bring life to people I come in contact with every day. With your strength, I will elevate others with encouragement and vision, in Jesus' name. Amen.

18

01 sun
02 mon
03 tue
04 wed
05 thu
06 fri
07 sat

But above all these things put on love, which is the bond of perfection.

COLOSSIANS 3:14

PUT ON

There are things that we "put on" every day. We put on our clothes, put on a coat, put on makeup, put on a retainer…. You get it. The truth is that there are times we don't always feel like "putting on" some of these things.

Love is the same way. We don't always feel like showing it. Love isn't a feeling. It's a choice we make for the good of others. That's exactly why God tells us to put it on whether we feel like it or not. So every morning, wake up, get out of bed, and put on love.

COMMITMENT PRAYER

Father, I believe that love is not a feeling I wait for but a decision I make to give the best I have to others. With Your grace, I put on love in my words and actions daily, in Jesus' name. Amen.

19

01 sun
02 mon
03 tue
04 wed
05 thu
06 fri
07 sat

"And the King will answer and say to them, 'Assuredly, I say to you, inasmuch as you did it to one of the least of these My brethren, you did it to Me.'"

MATTHEW 25:40

WORTH

My wife, Cathy, and I have three boys whom we love more than life itself. We would do anything necessary to protect them from anyone who would even think of harming them. If someone were to commit injustice against them, that person may as well do it to me.

This is the same kind of jealous love and care God has for all His children. Because of this powerful truth, we must be respectful and considerate of all people, regardless of how different they may be from us.

COMMITMENT PRAYER

Father, help me to remember that Your Son, Jesus, died for every person I meet. Every one of them was worthy of His life and blood. I commit to treat all people with the worth You have shown them, in Jesus' name. Amen.

20

01 sun
02 mon
03 tue
04 wed
05 thu
06 fri
07 sat

"Be angry, and do not sin": do not let the sun go down on your wrath, nor give place to the devil.

EPHESIANS 4:26,27

CONTROL

I play hockey, which is a very rough, physical game. A few years ago, my opponent took the opportunity to allow his stick to have fellowship with my face. Needless to say, I was a tad bit angry. Unfortunately, I didn't channel my anger very well. I introduced him to my stick! And it wasn't long before both of us were kicked out of the game.

The Bible says we can be angry and not sin. Anger can be a powerfully motivating emotion, if it is channeled into productive responses. I should have used my anger in that game to score the winning goal for my team.

Never allow your anger to turn to wrath against another person. Control your emotions and respond in the way that is best for everyone concerned.

COMMITMENT PRAYER

Father, thank You for Your longsuffering and grace in me to control my anger and emotions. Help me let anger be fuel to do the right thing with even greater passion than before, in Jesus' name. Amen.

21

01 sun
02 mon
03 tue
04 wed
05 thu
06 fri
07 sat

For you were bought at a price; therefore glorify God in your body and in your spirit, which are God's.

1 CORINTHIANS 6:20

FOR SALE

While in your favorite shopping center, you see that thing you've wanted for months. You look at the price, make the purchase, use it for a few months, and then get something new.

That's fine for material objects, but you and I are different. There are many young people who have "For Sale" signs around their necks. If others pay them the right compliments or special attention, they can buy their bodies and future.

Take the sign off your neck. The blood of Jesus has already purchased you. Don't sell out to sin. One day you will give yourself to your God-ordained marriage partner, and you'll be glad you waited!

COMMITMENT PRAYER

Father, I believe You have called me to glorify You in my heart and in my body. I belong to You, in Jesus' name. Amen.

22

01 sun
02 mon
03 tue
04 wed
05 thu
06 fri
07 sat

Do not be deceived, God is not mocked; for whatever a man sows, that he will also reap.

GALATIANS 6:7

HOLLYWOOD

Without question, one of the greatest influences on our minds today is Hollywood. Unfortunately, most television show producers and moviemakers are not really concerned about reality and truth. While the majority of physically intimate relationships played out on the screen are between unmarried people, rarely do we ever see these partners dealing with such consequences as guilt, sexual diseases, or unwanted pregnancy.

Unlike the lives of the characters on the screen, ours can't be fixed with a quick rewrite of a script. We must be prepared to live with the harvest of the seeds we've sown. When we sow seeds of sin, we will reap a harvest of death. But when we sow seeds of purity, faith, and integrity, we will be able to enjoy a harvest of blessings.

COMMITMENT PRAYER

Father, thank You for giving me the wisdom each day to think beyond the moment and to the long-term results of all my actions. I determine to sow good seeds to reap a good harvest, in Jesus' name. Amen.

23

01 sun
02 mon
03 tue
04 wed
05 thu
06 fri
07 sat

Flee sexual immorality. Every sin that a man does is outside the body, but he who commits sexual immorality sins against his own body.

1 CORINTHIANS 6:18

COKE

One night at Oneighty®, I pulled out a can of Coca-Cola and offered a slug to all. The Coke was passed around from one student to another until there was only one gulp left. "Who wants to finish it off?" I asked. Everyone knew what was left: backwash! And even worse, it was *junior high* backwash! No one wanted any part of it.

Then I pulled out a fresh can of Coke that had been sitting in a cooler of ice. I said, "Who wants to drink this entire untouched Coke all by yourself?" Students began to scream for the opportunity.

Here was my point. When you guard your body from sexual immorality, one day when you are married you'll be like a fresh can of Coke for your spouse. You won't have to enter the most important relationship of your life polluted with spiritual, emotional, and physical backwash.

COMMITMENT PRAYER

Father, I commit to keep my body pure. I will protect myself from the consequences of the sin of sexual immorality, in Jesus' name. Amen.

24

01 sun
02 mon
03 tue
04 wed
05 thu
06 fri
07 sat

And do not lead us into temptation,
but deliver us from the evil one....

MATTHEW 6:13

TEMPTATION

Recently a friend of mine was desperately trying to lose weight. His desire was very sincere, but he had one major problem: He worked at an ice cream shop every day! Even worse, his favorite food was ice cream!

I told him he would likely have better results in his weight loss program if he went out and got a job selling something he wasn't tempted to eat—perhaps electronics or something.

If you are dealing with temptation in the area of lust, you must employ the same kind of wisdom. Stay clear of people, magazines, Web sites, or anything else that will cause you to stumble. Be smart about where you go and what you see!

COMMITMENT PRAYER

Father, I believe You are giving me a discerning heart each day to lead me away from tempting circumstances and to deliver me from evil. In Jesus' name, I pray. Amen.

25

01 sun
02 mon
03 tue
04 wed
05 thu
06 fri
07 sat

Now concerning the things of which you wrote to me: It is good for a man not to touch a woman.

1 CORINTHIANS 7:1

TOUCH

I was seventeen years old when I first read this interesting Scripture. I ran to my youth pastor and told him I had sinned. He asked what I meant. I told him, "I've touched women," and went on to explain I regularly shook their hands, patted their backs, and even hugged some of them.

He assured me this was not the kind of touch the Bible was talking about. He showed me that the original word for "touch" in this verse did not refer to a casual or friendly touch. It literally meant a sensual touch that stirred up carnal fires in another person.

I finally got it: Stay away from any touch that you know can lead to increased physical intimacy.

COMMITMENT PRAYER

Father, thank You that Your Word is clear and provides definite standards, which I choose to live by each day. I submit myself to Your will for purity in my life, in Jesus' name. Amen.

26

01 sun
02 mon
03 tue
04 wed
05 thu
06 fri
07 sat

I wrote to you in my epistle not to keep company with sexually immoral people.

1 CORINTHIANS 5:9

BAD COMPANY

When we read this Scripture, our natural response is to think of those people we may know who are living sexually impure lives. But one night I challenged the young people at Oneighty® with this question: "What about the sexually immoral people you allow to speak into your life through television, movies, magazines, the Internet, and music?"

We must be careful to have discerning hearts and minds in choosing our entertainment "friends." Does their message stand in stark contrast to what we know to be true? If so, God says to part company with them.

COMMITMENT PRAYER

Father, thank You for giving me spiritual discernment in choosing my entertainment influences. I follow after truth and righteousness in all I watch and listen to, in Jesus' name. Amen.

27

01 sun
02 mon
03 tue
04 wed
05 thu
06 fri
07 sat

A fool vents all his feelings, but a wise man holds them back.

PROVERBS 29:11

FEELINGS

I remember that in my teenage years just about every girl I went out with I fell in love with—at least for a couple of weeks. The problem was that I would tell each one that I loved her. I would vocalize the first feeling that would find its way to my brain.

I had to learn to be guided by truth and wisdom rather than by feelings. Feelings can lie. Feelings come and go. A wise man will not allow his feelings to speak for him but will carefully follow after truth.

Never share words or make commitments that you may regret in the days to come.

COMMITMENT PRAYER

Father, help me to walk carefully in all my relationships. I will not vent my feelings but will hold them back and diligently follow truth, in Jesus' name. Amen.

28

01 sun
02 mon
03 tue
04 wed
05 thu
06 fri
07 sat

"You are of your father the devil, and the desires of your father you want to do. He was a murderer from the beginning, and does not stand in the truth, because there is no truth in him. When he speaks a lie, he speaks from his own resources, for he is a liar and the father of it."

JOHN 8:44

LIES

One of the largest lies ever perpetrated upon this generation of young people is the idea of "safe sex." That is, if you want to have promiscuous sex but don't want a sexual disease or a baby, just use "protection."

You could easily lump the lie of "safe sex" in with a host of others, such as "acceptable adultery," "charming cheating," "marvelous murder," or even "tasteful tax evasion."

We cannot try to mask or excuse behavior that is wrong. Let's reject the lies, no matter how well packaged they may come, and call those things what they really are: sin and abominations to our God.

COMMITMENT PRAYER

Heavenly Father, today I make a choice to reject all lies that Satan would try to slip into my mind. I choose to agree with Your Word, which is truth, in Jesus' name. Amen.

29

01 sun
02 mon
03 tue
04 wed
05 thu
06 fri
07 sat

Whoever falsely boasts of giving is like clouds and wind without rain.

PROVERBS 25:14

WITHOUT RAIN

Here in Oklahoma we recently came through a full summer month without rain. But there was something worse than the unbearable heat, the parched ground, and the burnt yellow lawns.

Clouds.

That's right, clouds! They would come, hang over our heads for a few hours, and leave. They hovered above us with a boastful promise of moisture and then left without a drop.

In relationships with others, don't ever say something that's not true or make a promise you can't deliver. Boastful deception and lies may make you look good in the short run but will always bring you to shame over the long haul.

COMMITMENT PRAYER

Heavenly Father, I am so secure in who You have made me that I don't need to boast falsely about myself. With Your help, I will always speak truthfully and honestly, in Jesus' name. Amen.

30

01	sun
02	mon
03	tue
04	wed
05	thu
06	fri
07	sat

But seek first the kingdom of God and His righteousness, and all these things shall be added to you.

MATTHEW 6:33

SEEK

I was eighteen years old. I wanted to get married really bad. I was looking hard and far for the one God had for me.

It was then that the Lord dealt with me to take one year and give it completely to Him without any dating at all. I thought it would be a difficult year, but it wasn't. God did so much in my life in that one year. He straightened out my priorities and gave me a defined purpose.

Just a few months after that year ended, I found my wife. She was literally the girl of my dreams: Six months before, I had dreamed I would marry her. She was beautiful, intelligent, and graceful in every way. There is no doubt I overachieved in my marriage to Cathy. When I put God first, He brought me His best.

Let God have your heart, and He will give you His desires for you.

COMMITMENT PRAYER

Heavenly Father, I commit to put You first in every area of my life, including my relationships. I won't seek after people or things. I seek You, in Jesus' name. Amen.

31

01 sun
02 mon
03 tue
04 wed
05 thu
06 fri
07 sat

Can a man take fire to his bosom, and his clothes not be burned?

PROVERBS 6:27

BURN

I stepped into the hospital room, and there lay the young man I'd been asked to visit and pray with. A mere shadow of his former self, he weighed just eighty-six pounds and was only days away from eternity.

I prayed with him, and he gave his life to Christ. He died three days later of AIDS. Shockingly, he'd had sexual contact with his girlfriend just once. Once! She'd had the HIV virus and had passed it on to him.

We cannot afford to play with the fires of sexual immorality. Sin and death have no friends or favorites. None of us can afford sin's heavy price.

COMMITMENT PRAYER

Father, thank You for opening my eyes to see the destructive nature of sin. I will not be deceived by its short-lived pleasures. I will walk in purity and goodness today, in Jesus' name. Amen.

32

01 sun
02 mon
03 tue
04 wed
05 thu
06 fri
07 sat

Do not be unequally yoked together with unbelievers. For what fellowship has righteousness with lawlessness? And what communion has light with darkness?

2 CORINTHIANS 6:14

ON TRACK

Back in the time in history when this Scripture was written, farmers would yoke together a team of oxen to plow a field. If one ox was stronger than the other, it would pull the plow off in the wrong direction. In order to keep the plow straight, a farmer had to pair together oxen of equal strength.

If you get paired with the wrong people, you can get pulled off track, too. Be sure you are yoked with friends of like faith and convictions.

COMMITMENT PRAYER

Father in heaven, I thank You for helping me to keep my life on track and in the right direction every day. I will yoke up with people who are heading in the same spiritual direction as I am, in Jesus' name. Amen.

33

01 sun
02 mon
03 tue
04 wed
05 thu
06 fri
07 sat

A friend loves at all times, and
a brother is born for adversity.

PROVERBS 17:17

TRUE FRIEND

For six years after he graduated from Manhattan's Fashion Institute of Technology, Calvin Klein could get nothing better than bad-paying jobs in New York's fashion district. He finally was ready to give up on fashion and look to the grocery industry with a family friend.

But that friend believed in young Calvin and gave him $10,000 in start-up money to start his own business. Today you can find Mr. Klein's name on clothing around the world.

A true friend will love and help you, even when you are at your lowest point.

COMMITMENT PRAYER

Father, thank You for Your love, which You have put within me. With Your help, I will use that love to encourage those around me, in Jesus' name. Amen.

34

01 sun
02 mon
03 tue
04 wed
05 thu
06 fri
07 sat

[Love] does not rejoice in iniquity,
but rejoices in the truth.

1 CORINTHIANS 13:6

BAD THINGS

Believe it or not, what I am about to tell you is a true story. A man walked into a convenience store, dropped a twenty-dollar bill on the counter, and asked for some change. When the employee opened the register, the man pulled out a gun and told the clerk to give him all the money. The thief quickly grabbed the cash and dashed, leaving his twenty-dollar bill on the counter.

The store profited five dollars in this transaction because there had been a total of just fifteen dollars in the drawer!

When we allow ourselves to do bad things in our relationships, bad things happen. We'll always end up on the short end when we take shortcuts by sinning.

COMMITMENT PRAYER

Father, I commit myself to purity and integrity in all my friendships. Thank You that I have Your power to resist every temptation to compromise, in Jesus' name I pray. Amen.

35

01 sun
02 mon
03 tue
04 wed
05 thu
06 fri
07 sat

[Love] does not behave rudely, does not seek its own, is not provoked, thinks no evil.

1 CORINTHIANS 13:5

BAD WEIGHT

A twenty-two-year-old from Dartmouth, Nova Scotia, came home from his bachelor party and accidentally plunged his vehicle into a lake. Unable to swim to the surface because of the weight of a ball and chain that had been attached to his leg by his friends at the party, he drowned.

Are you close to people who are rude, selfish, easily angered—even evil? They will eventually become a weight in your life that will drag you into areas you don't want to go to and may never return from.

COMMITMENT PRAYER

Father, thank You for helping me to produce the results of Your genuine love in my life every day. I am not selfish, rude, easily provoked, or evil in thought. In Jesus' name I pray. Amen.

36

01 sun
02 mon
03 tue
04 wed
05 thu
06 fri
07 sat

Love suffers long and is kind;
love does not envy; love does
not parade itself, is not puffed up.

1 CORINTHIANS 13:4

WHERE'S THE LOVE?

In Frederick, Maryland, a twenty-six-year-old shot and killed her boyfriend during an argument about which one of them loved the other more.

A true friend will not try to place himself above his friend in an effort to look better. In fact, envy and pride will eventually destroy any relationship.

Never allow yourself to compete with a friend for attention, respect, or anything else. If you do, you could drive a wedge between you and your friend and permanently destroy the future of your relationship.

COMMITMENT PRAYER

Heavenly Father, I thank You that Your love inside me is patient, kind, and does not envy or parade itself in pride. In Jesus' name I pray. Amen.

37

01 sun
02 mon
03 tue
04 wed
05 thu
06 fri
07 sat

My people are destroyed for lack of knowledge.

HOSEA 4:6

ROCKET SCIENCE

A recent study reported how adults say they first learned about sex. The majority said they learned first and foremost from other friends. The least likely source of their information about sex, according to this poll, was the church.

If you could ask NASA how to build and launch a rocket, would you ask your friends instead? If you did ask your friends, and you decided to take off in that rocket, it would likely be the final adventure of your life!

Similarly, it is important to understand that God created sex and He designed it to be between those in the covenant of marriage. It is critical that we look to His Word and teaching and not to the opinions of those unqualified to speak.

COMMITMENT PRAYER

Father, I will not allow my life and future to be destroyed by lacking knowledge about relationships. Give me ears to hear Your Word and a heart to act on what I know to be true, in Jesus' name I pray. Amen.

38

01 sun
02 mon
03 tue
04 wed
05 thu
06 fri
07 sat

Now hope does not disappoint, because the love of God has been poured out in our hearts by the Holy Spirit who was given to us.

ROMANS 5:5

BRING THEM

In the New Testament Gospels, Jesus personally and directly healed forty people. Of those forty, friends or family members brought thirty-four to Jesus, or brought Jesus to them. Just six of the forty made their way to Jesus by themselves, without someone else's help.

God has chosen to use us to show others what Jesus can do to heal their lives.

God's love is in you. Let it out.

COMMITMENT PRAYER

Heavenly Father, thank You that Your love is in my heart. I determine to allow that love to reach out to others every day, in Jesus' name. Amen.

39

01 sun
02 mon
03 tue
04 wed
05 thu
06 fri
07 sat

My brethren, do not hold the faith of our Lord Jesus Christ, the Lord of glory, with partiality.

JAMES 2:1

WITHOUT PREJUDICE

One night in the 1960s, a time of racial tension in this nation, an elderly African-American woman was standing on the side of an Alabama highway in a lashing rainstorm at 11:30 P.M. She was trying to find a ride because her car had broken down. A young white man stopped to help her—an act unheard of at this time. The man took her to safety and arranged for a taxi-cab to chauffeur her to her destination. She was in a hurry, but she wrote down the young man's address and thanked him.

Seven days later, there was a knock on the young man's door. To his surprise, a giant color TV was delivered to his home. Attached was a note thanking him for helping her get to her dying husband's bedside before he passed away. It was signed by Mrs. Nat King Cole, wife of the world-famous singer.

When we allow our love to be impartial, we will reach people we never thought we could.

COMMITMENT PRAYER

Father, thank You for giving me the ability to love all people all the time with a love that will never fail. In Jesus' name I pray. Amen.

40

01 sun
02 mon
03 tue
04 wed
05 thu
06 fri
07 sat

For I am not ashamed of the gospel of Christ, for it is the power of God to salvation for everyone who believes, for the Jew first and also for the Greek.

ROMANS 1:16

POWER SEEDS

As three young people were hanging out on a street corner, a Christian man came by to invite them to church. They came and, at his insistence, agreed to come back to his Sunday school class. They became the very core of his class every week.

Years later, a group of the man's friends decided to catch up with these boys to see what had become of them. They discovered that one had become a missionary to China, the second was the private secretary of President Herbert Hoover, and the third was President Hoover himself!

Every time you reach out to someone you plant a seed that has the potential to produce an unimaginable harvest.

COMMITMENT PRAYER

Father in heaven, I am not ashamed of the gospel of Jesus Christ. I will be bold to plant the seeds of love and truth in those I meet each day. In Jesus' name I pray. Amen.

41

01 sun
02 mon
03 tue
04 wed
05 thu
06 fri
07 sat

And let us consider one another in order to stir up love and good works.

HEBREWS 10:24

PEOPLE MAGNETS

Leadership expert John Maxwell often talks about the "law of magnetism." This law says, "Who you are is who you attract."[1] The thing that determines who will become your friends is not what you want but who you are.

Each day that you make choices based on the characteristics of honesty and truth, you provoke others by your actions to do the same. On the other hand, when you compromise and give in to sin, you attract people who will take you down even further.

The actions you choose to make each day determine the kind of people you attract. Choose wisely.

COMMITMENT PRAYER

Father, I make a choice today to allow my love and good works to stir up others to work for Your honor. Thank You for Your grace each step of the way, in Jesus' name. Amen.

42

01 sun
02 mon
03 tue
04 wed
05 thu
06 fri
07 sat

For the wages of sin is death, but the gift of God is eternal life in Christ Jesus our Lord.

ROMANS 6:23

BAD TRIP

One night, at the encouragement of her friends, a young lady made a bad decision. Returning from a bachelorette party aboard a chartered bus, she attempted to "moon" a passing car. The laughter stopped when she leaned up against the emergency window, which gave way and sent her tumbling onto the highway at fifty-five miles per hour.

Sometimes pressure from the wrong friends can cause you to do things that you would never do by yourself. Remember that sin always brings death. It's always wiser to seek to please God than to please people.

COMMITMENT PRAYER

Father, thank You for helping me to overcome all peer pressure in my life. My heart's desire is to always please You first, in Jesus' name. Amen.

43

01 sun
02 mon
03 tue
04 wed
05 thu
06 fri
07 sat

Rooted and built up in Him and established
in the faith, as you have been taught,
abounding in it with thanksgiving.

COLOSSIANS 2:7

GRATEFUL

Two old friends met each other on the street. One was down and depressed and when the other asked him why, he replied, "Let me tell you. Three weeks ago, an uncle died and left me $40,000."

"Wow! That's a lot of money!" said his friend.

"But you see, two weeks ago a cousin I never knew kicked the bucket and left me $85,000 free and clear."

"Sounds like you should be grateful."

"You don't understand!" he interrupted. "Last week, my great aunt passed away. I inherited almost a quarter of a million dollars."

Really confused by now, his old friend said, "Then why are you so glum?"

"This week, nothing!"

Unfortunately, some people value their possessions more than their friends and family. Never let that be said of you.

COMMITMENT PRAYER

Father, I am so thankful for all my friends and family. I pray that You will continue to bless and guide each one of them into all You have for them, in Jesus' name. Amen.

44

01 sun
02 mon
03 tue
04 wed
05 thu
06 fri
07 sat

Therefore, as we have opportunity,
let us do good to all, especially to those
who are of the household of faith.

GALATIANS 6:10

General William Westmoreland once reviewed a platoon of paratroopers in Vietnam. As he went down the line he asked each of them this question: "How do you like jumping, son?"

"Love it, sir!" was the first answer.

"The greatest experience in my life, sir!" shouted the next paratrooper.

"I hate it, sir," the third replied.

"Then why do you do it?" asked Westmoreland.

"Because I want to be around the guys who love to jump."

It's important that we stay close to those who are of "the household of faith," the church. That's where we are going to learn, grow, and experience God's goodness together. We must make a commitment to be around the right crowd.

COMMITMENT PRAYER

Father, thank You for my church. I trust that You will help me to continue to grow in my relationships with all of my brothers and sisters in the body of Christ, in Jesus' name. Amen.

45

01 sun
02 mon
03 tue
04 wed
05 thu
06 fri
07 sat

What then shall we say to these things?
If God is for us, who can be against us?

ROMANS 8:31

BELIEVE

A professional public speaker was recently quoted as saying, "My friends didn't believe that I could become a successful speaker. So I did something about it. I went out and found me some new friends!"

The truth is, God is for us and nobody can stand against us. You must believe in yourself and surround yourself with people who believe in you as well. We never get to the peak of our potential alone. We must have a strong group of peers who help us get there.

COMMITMENT PRAYER

Heavenly Father, I believe that You are accomplishing great things in my life. I commit to have faith in those plans each day, in Jesus' name. Amen.

46

01 sun
02 mon
03 tue
04 wed
05 thu
06 fri
07 sat

Even a fool is counted wise when he holds
his peace; when he shuts his lips,
he is considered perceptive.

PROVERBS 17:28

LISTEN UP

A great American leadership and management trainer recently said, "In hundreds of interviews with people at all levels I've made this discovery: The bigger the person, the more apt he is to encourage you to talk; the smaller the person, the more apt he is to preach to you. Big people monopolize the listening; small people monopolize the talking!"

There's a reason God gave us two ears and one mouth. Good leaders are great listeners, as are good friends. Are you more concerned with hearing or being heard?

COMMITMENT PRAYER.

Father, thank You for helping me to be a graceful listener to those around me. I know that the more I listen, the more I'll learn. In Jesus' name I pray. Amen.

47

01 sun
02 mon
03 tue
04 wed
05 thu
06 fri
07 sat

Better to dwell in a corner of a housetop, Than in a house shared with a contentious woman.

PROVERBS 21:9

BAD SEEDS

A man named Max Jukes lived in the state of New York. He did not believe in providing Christian upbringing and training for his children. He married a girl of like character. From this union came 1,026 descendants. This is what happened to them:

- Three hundred died prematurely.
- One hundred went to the penitentiary for an average of thirteen years each.
- Ninety were public prostitutes.
- Ten were drunkards.
- The family cost the state $1,200,000.
- They made no positive contribution to society.[2]

Proverbs tells us to get far away from those who are contentious. We should stay far away from those who are not showing the fruit of the Spirit. From this illustration we see clearly that bad relationships produce bad results.

COMMITMENT PRAYER

Father, I thank You that my friendships and relationships will produce godly fruit and results. In Jesus' name I pray. Amen.

48

01 sun
02 mon
03 tue
04 wed
05 thu
06 fri
07 sat

Train up a child in the way he should go,
And when he is old he will not depart from it.

PROVERBS 22:6

GOOD SEEDS

Jonathon Edwards lived in New York, as did Max Jukes. However, unlike Mr. Jukes, Mr. Edwards believed in Christian training and married a girl of like character. From this union came 729 descendants. This is what happened to them:

- Three hundred became preachers.
- Sixty-five were college professors.
- Thirteen became university presidents.
- Sixty were authors of good books.
- Three became United States congressmen.
- One was the vice president of the United States.[3]

Except for Aaron Burr, a grandson of Edwards who married a woman of questionable character, the family did not cost the state a single dollar.

When we submit to the right influences in our lives, the right things happen.

COMMITMENT PRAYER

Father, I am careful to receive correction, direction, and influence from the right sources. I will make the right decisions, in Jesus' name. Amen.

49

01 sun
02 mon
03 tue
04 wed
05 thu
06 fri
07 sat

Not forsaking the assembling of ourselves together, as is the manner of some, but exhorting one another, and so much the more as you see the Day approaching.

HEBREWS 10:25

PLUGGED IN

It is a proven fact that when a person isolates himself from people, he is two to three times more likely to die an early death, even if he takes good care of himself by exercising and not smoking.

This is just one of the reasons that the Word of God admonishes us to gather together regularly with those of like, precious faith. Stay plugged in to your home church each and every week!

COMMITMENT PRAYER

Father, in Jesus' name, I pray for my church, my pastor, and my congregation. Thank You for helping me to find my assignment in the church of the Lord Jesus Christ. Amen.

50

01 sun
02 mon
03 tue
04 wed
05 thu
06 fri
07 sat

But now indeed there are many members, yet one body.

1 CORINTHIANS 12:20

TOGETHER

A great woman of God affectionately known around the world as Mother Teresa gave her life to reaching, feeding, and loving the most impoverished people of India. She was a frail-looking woman, but her convictions were as strong as steel. She once said, "I can do what you can't do, and you can do what I can't do. Together we can do great things."

This is the wonderful truth of the body of Christ. Even a great person like Mother Teresa couldn't do her work alone. We are meant to support and complement one another, each of us obeying God and doing his part.

COMMITMENT PRAYER

Father in heaven, thank You that I don't have to stand alone. I ask You to connect me to the right people in the right places for the right things, in Jesus' name. Amen.

51

01 sun
02 mon
03 tue
04 wed
05 thu
06 fri
07 sat

Though one may be overpowered by another, two can withstand him. And a threefold cord is not quickly broken.

ECCLESIASTES 4:12

ASSOCIATION

Maybe you know someone who drives a Ford automobile. Of course, it's a well-known fact that Mr. Henry Ford, the founder of Ford Motor Company overcame great odds to make himself one of the richest men in America. However, many are not aware that Mr. Ford's greatest strides came after forming close personal friendships with men of great mental capacity, such as Thomas A. Edison, Harvey Firestone, John Buttoughs, and Luther Burbank.

We take on the nature, habits, and power of thought of those with whom we associate.

COMMITMENT PRAYER

Father, I thank You that there is a multiplication of power and ability when I unite in purpose with the godly friends You bring into my life. In Jesus' name I pray. Amen.

52

01 sun
02 mon
03 tue
04 wed
05 thu
06 fri
07 sat

Now I plead with you, brethren, by the name of our Lord Jesus Christ, that you all speak the same thing, and that there be no divisions among you, but that you be perfectly joined together in the same mind and in the same judgment.

1 CORINTHIANS 1:10

CONNECTED

Do you remember playing with Lego's when you were a kid? It probably wasn't that long ago, was it? Well, you can fit together two eight-stud bricks in twenty-four different ways. Three of them will fit together in 1,060 ways. But six of those same eight-stud bricks offer 102,981,500 opportunities for connection!

The more good, strong spiritual connections we make in our relationships, the stronger the walls of what we construct in life will be. And in the end, we will have built a tower that serves as a model to the next generation.

COMMITMENT PRAYER

Father in heaven, thank You for helping me to make all the right connections in my life. Let my connections be pure, strong, and productive for the kingdom of God, in Jesus' name. Amen.

53

01 sun
02 mon
03 tue
04 wed
05 thu
06 fri
07 sat

Debate your case with your neighbor,
and do not disclose the secret to another.

PROVERBS 25:9

TRUST

Without a doubt, one of the best-selling newspapers in the nation is *The National Enquirer.* Feeding the dark elements of human nature, it exposes people's personal secrets to the whole world. While "rag-mags" like this one sell very well, I doubt any of their reporters are very proud of what they do. And I'm sure they wouldn't want anyone to do a front-page exposé of their private lives!

Let's not engage in "National Enquirer" relationships with others. There are confidences that friends are meant to keep. I'm not talking about hiding or covering up sin—especially not sin that harms others. I'm simply saying if you want to keep your friends, learn to be trustworthy.

COMMITMENT PRAYER

Father, thank You for giving me wisdom to build trust and integrity in all my relationships. With Your help, I will be a true friend to others, in Jesus' name. Amen.

54

01 sun
02 mon
03 tue
04 wed
05 thu
06 fri
07 sat

Go therefore and make disciples of all the nations, baptizing them in the name of the Father and of the Son and of the Holy Spirit.

MATTHEW 28:19

DISCIPLINE

A church researcher recently studied fifteen different churches that had at least twelve new converts in the past year. His findings proved that if a new convert developed at least seven Christian friendships in the first six months, he remained strong with God and his church. If, however, he had three or fewer Christian friendships, he would almost always fall back into his old life.

As Christians, we have to learn to disciple new Christians. Call them up, take them to church, teach them the Word, pray with them, and, most of all, help them build new relationships in the body of Christ.

COMMITMENT PRAYER

Father, thank You for helping me to take responsibility to reach out and strengthen new believers. In Jesus' name I pray. Amen.

55

01 sun
02 mon
03 tue
04 wed
05 thu
06 fri
07 sat

Flee also youthful lusts; but pursue righteousness, faith, love, peace with those who call on the Lord out of a pure heart.

2 TIMOTHY 2:22

RUN

A large secular American medical organization did a study on how to avoid sexual disease. After spending $6 million on research, they came to the following conclusion: To assure strong health and freedom from sexual disease, a person who wants to be sexually active must maintain a monogamous marriage relationship.

They could have saved $5,999,990 by buying and reading a $10 Bible! The very reason God's Word warns against pursuing lust and premarital sex is for our own protection and peace of mind. Run from lust, and run after righteousness.

COMMITMENT PRAYER

Heavenly Father, I believe You have given me Your commandments for my good and benefit. My heart and mind are focused on Your Word and plan for my future, in Jesus' name. Amen.

56

01 sun
02 mon
03 tue
04 wed
05 thu
06 fri
07 sat

My little children, let us not love in word
or in tongue, but in deed and in truth.

1 JOHN 3:18

ACTION

I was shocked when I read this statistic. According to a national study of teenagers, religious-conscious girls were 86 percent more likely to say it's important to be a virgin when married than were non-religious girls. But here's where my alarm kicked in. These same religious-conscious girls were only 14 percent more likely to actually be virgins when married than were non-religious girls.

Translation: Many Christian young people believe in sexual purity, but their beliefs are not always resulting in action. The Bible commands us to be sure that our actions match what we say we believe. Are you living what you believe?

COMMITMENT PRAYER

Heavenly Father, thank You for Your ability in me to back up my words and conviction with actions that honor You. In Jesus' name I pray. Amen.

Make the Zero Pledge

Lord, I make this solemn pledge before you right now. Zero compromise. Starting today I will not compromise in my relationships with others. I will not allow myself to be unequally yoked in a friendship with an unbeliever. I will keep myself pure with the help and grace of God. In Jesus' name. Amen.

Oneighty.Me

The Bible commands each of us to love his neighbor as he loves himself. Well, this instruction begins with the foundation of loving ourselves first. That would be "me." I am not talking about developing an attitude of selfishness, but rather about learning to operate with a healthy self-esteem.

It is important that you highly esteem the person God has made you and greatly value what He has called you to do. A holy confidence will enable you to relate more effectively with those around you. As you read through this daily devotional series, get ready to take your faith to a brand-new level! Go ahead. Turn the page, and let's get started.

//oneighty.me

03

01

01 sun
02 mon
03 tue
04 wed
05 thu
06 fri
07 sat

"You shall love your neighbor as yourself."

MATTHEW 19:19

LOVE

I am well known among my friends and family for letting my car run out of gas. I'm always pushing the fuel tank to its limit, and sometimes I end up on the side of the road waiting for my wife, Cathy, to show up with a can of gas.

The love of God is a critical fuel in your life. You can't give something that you don't have to someone else. You must love yourself with God's love before you'll ever be able to really love someone else. That simply means that you need to respect all that God has put inside you and choose His best for your life at all times.

Stop running on empty. Choose to receive all that God wants to fill you with.

COMMITMENT PRAYER

Father, thank You that Your love has been shed abroad in my heart. I choose to make decisions that will result in Your best for me each day, in Jesus' name. Amen.

02

01 sun
02 mon
03 tue
04 wed
05 thu
06 fri
07 sat

What then shall we say to these things?
If God is for us, who can be against us?

ROMANS 8:31

GOLD

I wrote this Scripture on both of my skis as a constant reminder that God was for me. Each weekend as I would ride up on the chair lift in Banff, Alberta, I would look down and think about God's power that was always there to help me.

It wasn't long before I won my first gold medal in freestyle snow skiing, becoming the provincial aerial champion.

No matter what kind of competition or obstacle stands before you, there is Someone even bigger and stronger backing you up. Write that promise down somewhere so you'll never forget it.

COMMITMENT PRAYER

Father, I know that if You are for me, no one can possibly stand against me. I will not give in to fear or intimidation, in Jesus' name. Amen.

03

01 sun
02 mon
03 tue
04 wed
05 thu
06 fri
07 sat

For God has not given us a spirit of fear, but of power and of love and of a sound mind.

2 TIMOTHY 1:7

FEAR

A circus lion tamer was doing a performance in a large cage full of lions. In the middle of his presentation the arena lost power and the lights went out for more than thirty seconds.

People began to panic, but when the lights came back on they were amazed to see the lion tamer controlling the lions with his whip and confident speech. Workers quickly removed the lion tamer from the cage and asked him how he had managed to keep the lions under control while in the dark. He said, "Lions have very good night vision. They could see every move I made. They didn't know I couldn't see them."

When fear tries to grip your heart and mind, remember it isn't from God. You can stand confidently as you face fear, knowing that God is on your side.

COMMITMENT PRAYER

Lord, thank You for giving me a spirit of power, love, and a sound mind. I have more confidence in You and Your power in me than in the problems that try to stand against me. In Jesus' name, I pray. Amen.

04

01 sun
02 mon
03 tue
04 wed
05 thu
06 fri
07 sat

That the sharing of your faith may become effective by the acknowledgment of every good thing which is in you in Christ Jesus.

PHILEMON 1:6

SHARE

I have the privilege of playing hockey in an adult league each week alongside former NHL all-star Gary Unger. Needless to say, hockey has been very good to Gary and his wonderful family. He is always sharing great hockey stories on the bench and in the dressing room. At fifty-something years old, he still loves it!

Do you want to share your faith in Christ in a great way? Take time to open God's Word to both discover and experience all the good things He's promised to you if you'll believe. When you are enjoying God's incredible goodness, you can't help but tell others all about it!

COMMITMENT PRAYER

Father, thank You for the good things You have promised me in Your Word. I believe in and receive all that You have for me, in Jesus' name. Amen.

05

01 sun
02 mon
03 tue
04 wed
05 thu
06 fri
07 sat

And He said to them, "Go into all the world and preach the gospel to every creature."

MARK 16:15

JOY

The New Testament Gospels record accounts of Jesus' healing forty people during His ministry on earth. Of those forty different people, only six found their way to Jesus on their own. Friends, family, or others brought the remaining thirty-four to Jesus.

Few people find Jesus on their own. God wants to use you to help others get to know Him. The best way to introduce people to Jesus is to let them see Jesus in you. Let your life, your actions, and your words reveal God's love and character. Jesus said, "You are the salt of the earth." Let your life make others want a taste of what you have.

COMMITMENT PRAYER

Lord, show me people in my world whom I can lead to You. Give me the courage to share Your words, and help me live the life that backs them up, in Jesus' name. Amen.

06

01 sun
02 mon
03 tue
04 wed
05 thu
06 fri
07 sat

For the wages of sin is death, but the gift of God is eternal life in Christ Jesus our Lord.

ROMANS 6:23

BITES

One evening, as a young man was giving his pet scorpion its usual good night kiss, the scorpion grabbed the man's lips with his pinchers. Then it jumped inside his mouth and returned the kiss by stabbing the man's tongue with his stinger.

If you kiss a scorpion often enough, eventually you will get stung. And if you play with sin enough, sooner or later it, too, will sting you.

Stay away from sinful influences that could lead you from God. Sin looks friendly and inviting at first, but in the end it is a killer. Sin has only one purpose: to destroy your dreams, crush your heart, and separate you from God.

Avoid getting stung. Stay away from sin and its influences.

COMMITMENT PRAYER

Heavenly Father, open my eyes to see the dangers of sin. I choose to flee youthful lust and to pursue righteousness and integrity, in Jesus' name. Amen.

07

01 sun
02 mon
03 tue
04 wed
05 thu
06 fri
07 sat

He who observes the wind will not sow, and he who regards the clouds will not reap.

ECCLESIASTES 11:4

DREAMS

A young boy was badly burned on the lower half of his body while unsuccessfully trying to save his little brother's life during a school fire. Doctors said he would never walk again. Every day he would sit on the front porch watching the children run and play. Determined to walk again, he pulled himself out of his wheelchair, dragged himself to the fence, and dragged his body the distance of the fence and back as his lifeless leg hung limp.

Eventually, feeling began to return to his leg and he was able to walk to school. Then he ran to school. He later joined the college track team. Eventually this young man named Glen Cunningham became the first human in recorded history to break the four-minute mile.

This young boy made no excuses. He pushed himself hard. And eventually he achieved his dream. You can too.

COMMITMENT PRAYER

Father in heaven, no obstacle is too big for You. With Your strength, I pursue the dream You have given me and I cannot fail, in Jesus' name. Amen.

08

01 sun
02 mon
03 tue
04 wed
05 thu
06 fri
07 sat

But you, beloved, building yourselves up on
your most holy faith, praying in the Holy Spirit.

JUDE 1:20

STRENGTH

I lift weights three to four times every week. There are times I look forward to it and times I have no desire at all. Regardless of how I feel, every time I push iron over my head it helps to strengthen my body. And over time, I can both feel and see the difference.

The same is true with prayer. There will be times when you feel like praying and lots of times when you don't. But it makes no difference. With or without feelings, when you pray the Word of God over your life, you will be built up and strengthened spiritually.

COMMITMENT PRAYER

Heavenly Father, I believe in the power of prayer. I thank You for strengthening me each day as I pray the Word of God over my life, in Jesus' name. Amen.

09

01 sun
02 mon
03 tue
04 wed
05 thu
06 fri
07 sat

Looking carefully lest anyone fall short of the grace of God; lest any root of bitterness springing up cause trouble, and by this many become defiled.

HEBREWS 12:15

BITTERNESS

Benedict Arnold was one of America's best generals in the Continental Army during the Revolutionary War. But he was continually passed over at reviews so that congressmen could promote their favorite sons. He allowed bitterness to take so much root in his heart that he eventually betrayed his country.

Today if you visit West Point Military Academy you can see a wall of plaques and paintings honoring the senior officers of the Revolutionary War. General George Washington's picture is in the center and most prominent place. But off in an obscure corner you will find a small plaque with this engraving: "Major General DOB 1741." In place of Benedict Arnold's name is simply a chiseled blank space.

Don't risk missing your place in history by allowing bitterness in your heart. When life isn't fair, don't react with insecurity and bitterness. Respond with trust that God will reward you.

COMMITMENT PRAYER

Heavenly Father, I choose not to hold bitterness in my heart toward others but to forgive them, just as You have forgiven me. When life and people aren't fair toward me, I trust You to protect me, in Jesus' name. Amen.

10

01 sun
02 mon
03 tue
04 wed
05 thu
06 fri
07 sat

Do not be deceived, God is not mocked; for whatever a man sows, that he will also reap.

GALATIANS 6:7

LIFT

Look at some of these creative cut-downs and see if you have ever been guilty of using them: "You got into the gene pool when the lifeguard wasn't watching." "If I gave you a penny for your thoughts, you'd get change." "When you open your mouth it seems that it's only to change whatever foot was previously in there."

Small people cut others down to feel good about themselves. A person with a healthy self-esteem doesn't need to.

If you want to feel good, help someone else feel good. Reach out. Be a friend. Give a kind word. Be the bigger person: Lift others up to your level rather than cutting them down.

COMMITMENT PRAYER

Father, help me to speak only words that build others up. Use me to lift others closer to You, in Jesus' name. Amen.

11

01 sun
02 mon
03 tue
04 wed
05 thu
06 fri
07 sat

Casting down arguments and every high thing that exalts itself against the knowledge of God, bringing every thought into captivity to the obedience of Christ.

2 CORINTHIANS 10:5

GATE

Years ago the people of China feared invasion, so they built the Great Wall of China. This wall extends 1500 miles. It is so large that one can see it from a space orbit around earth. The wall is so high and wide that it is virtually impregnable to land attack.

However, after the first 100 years of the wall's completion, China was invaded three times. How did the enemy get in? They didn't climb over the wall, dig under it, or blast through it. They simply bribed the gatekeepers to let them through.

Keep Satan out of your life by keeping the gate of your mind closed to his tempting bribes. Tell him your mind is not for sale!

COMMITMENT PRAYER

Heavenly Father, I will take every thought captive to make sure it is obedient to God's Word. May the meditation of my heart and mind be pleasing in Your sight, in Jesus' name. Amen.

12

01 sun
02 mon
03 tue
04 wed
05 thu
06 fri
07 sat

So then faith comes by hearing, and
hearing by the word of God.

ROMANS 10:17

FAITH

Shortly after I graduated from Bible college, God gave me a dream
to reach a nation of teenagers with a television program that
proclaimed Christ in a creative and innovative way. I remained in
obscurity for years but continued to speak the Word of God over
my dreams and future. The more I spoke the Word of God, the
stronger my faith became.

When I was twenty-six years old we launched *Fire by Nite,* the first Christian television program
of its kind. It combined drama, comedy sketches, music, and preaching. It would be aired
worldwide for more that ten years. Today, I can't go to a city without someone stopping me and
telling me how they came to Christ through *Fire by Nite.*

Speak the Word of God over your life and dreams every day. Expect great things, and you'll
see them!

COMMITMENT PRAYER

Father, I thank You for putting Your dreams in my heart. I believe and speak the Word boldly
about those dreams and am confident You are bringing them to pass, in Jesus' name. Amen.

13

01 sun	
02 mon	
03 tue	
04 wed	
05 thu	
06 fri	
07 sat	

Thus says the Lord, your Redeemer, the Holy One of Israel: "I am the Lord your God, Who teaches you to profit, Who leads you by the way you should go."

ISAIAH 48:17

OPPORTUNITY

A twenty-three-year-old trash collector in Massachusetts was working on his route when he noticed a Wendy's contest cup sitting in the trash. The previous week he had won a chicken sandwich, so he thought he would give it another try. When he peeled back the contest game piece he was amazed to see "Congratulations. You have won $200,000." Wow! That's not a bad day at the office!

In His Word God has given us promises far bigger and better than any Wendy's cup has to offer. Don't leave your opportunities unopened. Spend a few minutes every day reading God's Word to find all the great things He has in store for you.

COMMITMENT PRAYER

Lord, I don't take for granted Your exceedingly great and precious promises. Thank You that through them I have everything I need to live a successful and godly life, in Jesus' name. Amen.

14

01 sun
02 mon
03 tue
04 wed
05 thu
06 fri
07 sat

Let this mind be in you which was
also in Christ Jesus.

PHILIPPIANS 2:5

SUCCESS

Some negative people got together to offer these pessimistic poster suggestions: "Eagles may soar, but weasels don't get sucked into jet engines." "Doing the job right the first time gets the job done, but doing it wrong fourteen times provides job security." "Team: It means never having to take all the blame yourself."

These may be humorous, but unfortunately they reflect the negative attitude of so many Americans. A Fortune 500 study found that 94 percent of all corporate executives attribute their success to a positive attitude. Develop a positive, Christlike attitude, and you will outshine the crowd.

COMMITMENT PRAYER

Heavenly Father, I desire to have the same attitude Christ had when He came to this earth: the attitude of a servant. Let my life radiate Your joy, confidence, and love, in Jesus' name. Amen.

15

01 sun
02 mon
03 tue
04 wed
05 thu
06 fri
07 sat

Happy is the man who finds wisdom, and the man who gains understanding; for her proceeds are better than the profits of silver, and her gain than fine gold.

PROVERBS 3:13,14

WISDOM

Years ago in Greece a young student of philosophy asked his teacher how to gain wisdom. His wise, old teacher said, "Follow me, and I will show you." He took his pupil to the seashore and told him to wade into the water. Then he placed his hands on the student's head and pushed him under. Desperate for air, the student began to squirm to break free. After a long moment the teacher released the student, who launched out gasping for air.

The wise, old teacher calmly said, "When you want wisdom as badly as you wanted air—more than anything else—you will get it."

How badly do you want your dreams? If you will be passionate about fulfilling the dreams that God has placed in your heart, they will become a reality.

COMMITMENT PRAYER

Heavenly Father, I will seek Your wisdom as silver and search for it as for treasure, in Jesus' name. Amen.

16

01 sun
02 mon
03 tue
04 wed
05 thu
06 fri
07 sat

Now to Him who is able to do exceedingly abundantly above all that we ask or think, according to the power that works in us.

EPHESIANS 3:20

ACTIVATE

Cathy Hunt was not only great looking and the most popular girl in the school, but she was also a strong Christian. Every guy in the school—even I—wanted to take her out. All the way through high school, she would have nothing to do with me. I didn't stand a chance, or so I thought.

One year after graduation, God supernaturally brought us together through an unusual series of events. We were married a few months later. Honestly, I would never have either asked or even thought that the Lord would give me such a wonderful woman.

If you are a born-again believer, then you serve a God who gives more than you would ever think of or ask for. When you activate His power inside by believing and speaking His Word, your life will be better than you could ever imagine.

COMMITMENT PRAYER

Heavenly Father, I choose today to activate the power of God in me by praying Your Word. I fully believe that You will do beyond what I could ever think or ask, in Jesus' name. Amen.

17

01 sun
02 mon
03 tue
04 wed
05 thu
06 fri
07 sat

But the word of the Lord endures forever.

1 PETER 1:25

ROCK

An old urban legend tells the story of this radio conversation between a Navy vessel and a civilian.

Navy: This is the aircraft carrier Enterprise. We are a large warship of the U.S. Navy. Divert your course fifteen degrees to the north to avoid a collision.

Civilian: Recommend you divert your course fifteen degrees to the south to avoid a collision. This is a lighthouse. Your call.

God's laws are like that lighthouse. Some say they're outdated and old fashioned. They can say what they want and ignore their warnings, but that doesn't make them go away. God's Word will last forever. You can either listen to its warnings and walk by its light, or ignore it and be crushed against the jagged rocks of life. Your call.

COMMITMENT PRAYER

Father, I will build my life upon the rock of Your Word. Thank You that Your Word helps me stand firm in the midst of storms, in Jesus' name. Amen.

18

01 sun
02 mon
03 tue
04 wed
05 thu
06 fri
07 sat

An inheritance gained hastily at the beginning will not be blessed at the end.

PROVERBS 20:21

FIRST

A man in a hurry to get rich spent all his money on lottery tickets. He then began to embezzle money from his workplace to buy more tickets. Over time he embezzled over $500,000, only to win a total of $2500, which he spent on more losing lottery tickets. He eventually was caught and sent to jail. Stealing not only put him in prison but cost him his freedom, career, and family.

Some people mistakenly believe that the way to get ahead in life is by stealing from others, but stealing always ends up hurting the thief. Don't be pressured into getting rich quickly through dishonesty. Follow God's plan to prosperity, the first step of which is honesty.

COMMITMENT PRAYER

Father, Your Word says You desire to bless and prosper me in every area of my life. I choose to follow Your path to success that lasts forever, in Jesus' name. Amen.

19

01 sun
02 mon
03 tue
04 wed
05 thu
06 fri
07 sat

He who dwells in the secret place of the Most High shall abide under the shadow of the Almighty.

PSALM 91:1

WINGS

One time after a forest fire some park rangers climbed a mountain to assess the damages. One ranger saw at the base of a tree a large bird, petrified by the fire's ashes and smoke. The ranger knocked the bird over with a stick, and three tiny chicks scurried from under its wings. The mother bird, who had been aware of the dangers of the fire, could have flown away but instead sacrificed her life to save her baby chicks.

When problems mount up against you, don't panic or worry. God will protect you. Run to Him, and He will hide you under the shadow of His wings.

COMMITMENT PRAYER

Father, thank You for sending Your Son to lay down His life for me and to free me from sin and its consequences. I place my trust in You and dwell under the shadow of Your wings, in Jesus' name. Amen.

20

01 sun
02 mon
03 tue
04 wed
05 thu
06 fri
07 sat

For even when we were with you, we commanded you this: If anyone will not work, neither shall he eat.

2 THESSALONIANS 3:10

HANDOUTS

Years ago in Monterey, California, fishermen would pull their boats into the docks and clean their fish. They would feed the fish entrails to the pelicans that would hang around looking for handouts. After many years the fishing industry found a commercial use for the fish entrails and no longer tossed them to the pelicans. The fat and lazy pelicans who'd lived their whole lives on handouts had forgotten how to fish. Many of them starved to death waiting for another handout.

Don't build your life with the attitude that people owe you. Depend on God and work hard, and you will gain self-respect and achieve your dreams.

COMMITMENT PRAYER

Father, I choose to be diligent in the opportunities I have each day. I put my trust in You alone, in Jesus' name. Amen.

21

01 sun
02 mon
03 tue
04 wed
05 thu
06 fri
07 sat

Death and life are in the power of the tongue,
and those who love it will eat its fruit.

PROVERBS 18:21

TONGUE

I was just twelve years old, but I will never forget Yosh Senda. He was my judo coach at the local YMCA in Lethbridge, Alberta, where I practiced three to four times per week. Mr. Senda would always take me aside, point to an Olympics poster on the training room wall and tell me, "One day you're going to be an Olympic champion in judo."

As I would grow older, God would have a different direction for my life, but the impact of his faith in me was undeniable. I became a provincial judo champion several years in a row.

It's amazing what you can do when people believe in you.

Listen: God believes in you! And He has the power to help you reach your goals. He has given you His Word. When you speak it and believe it, you are bringing life to your future.

COMMITMENT PRAYER

Father, thank You for believing in me. I will use my tongue to speak Your Word and bring life to my future, in Jesus' name. Amen.

22

01 sun
02 mon
03 tue
04 wed
05 thu
06 fri
07 sat

There is therefore now no condemnation to those who are in Christ Jesus, who do not walk according to the flesh, but according to the Spirit.

ROMANS 8:1

PURSUE

Researchers placed four monkeys in a room that had a pole in the center with a banana bunch at the top. One monkey tried to climb the pole to get the bananas, but before he could reach them, a hose doused him with cold water. The second, third, and fourth monkeys tried but were also doused. The researchers then replaced one of the monkeys with a new one. This monkey saw the bananas and started to climb the pole, but the other three who had been doused ran and pulled him down. One by one the monkeys were replaced with new ones, until none of the monkeys in the room had ever been doused. But because they had been pulled down, they pulled the rest of the new monkeys down as well.

Beware of those who try to talk you out of your dream just because they've had bad experiences. Put your faith in God and His Word and pursue His dream for you.

COMMITMENT PRAYER

Father, show me any relationship that is hindering me from climbing higher. Help me surround myself with godly friends, in Jesus' name. Amen.

23

01 sun
02 mon
03 tue
04 wed
05 thu
06 fri
07 sat

Beloved, I pray that you may prosper in all things and be in health, just as your soul prospers.

3 JOHN 1:2

PROSPER

Here are seven signs that indicate you are really broke.

- American Express calls and says, "Leave home without it."
- You've rolled so many pennies, you've formed a bond with Abe Lincoln.
- You look at your roommate and see a large fried chicken in tennis shoes.
- You finally clean your room, hoping to find change.
- You give blood every day just for the orange juice.
- At communion you go back for seconds.
- Your bologna has no first name.

God wants to bless you just as parents want to see their children blessed with good things. True financial prosperity is a by-product of our being spiritually prosperous. Take time every day to read and meditate on God's Word, and you will be prosperous spiritually, emotionally, and financially.

COMMITMENT PRAYER

Father, I will meditate on Your Word and do all that is written in it. Thank You that You take great delight in my prosperity, in Jesus' name. Amen.

24

01 sun
02 mon
03 tue
04 wed
05 thu
06 fri
07 sat

Let no corrupt word proceed out of your mouth,
but what is good for necessary edification,
that it may impart grace to the hearers.

EPHESIANS 4:29

ENCOURAGER

A little girl came home from a tough day at school and collapsed onto the sofa in her living room. She sighed to herself out loud: "Nobody loves me. The whole world hates me!" Her little brother, who was in the room playing video games, responded, "That's not true, Sis. Some people don't even know you."

He'd had a great opportunity to give some encouraging words to his sister, but instead he'd only added to her frustrations.

If you want people to seek you out as a friend, then be an encourager. It takes a great person to see past people's shortcomings to find the good things and praise them.

COMMITMENT PRAYER

Father, I will not let negative or unwholesome words out of my mouth but only words that lift others closer to You. In Jesus' name, I pray. Amen.

25

01 sun
02 mon
03 tue
04 wed
05 thu
06 fri
07 sat

But you are a chosen generation, a royal priesthood, a holy nation, His own special people, that you may proclaim the praises of Him who called you out of darkness into His marvelous light.

1 PETER 2:9

DIFFERENCE

A gentleman noticed a boy picking up starfish and tossing them into the sea. He approached the boy and asked why. The boy said, "If the starfish were left on the shore until morning they would die."

The curious gentleman asked, "How can your small effort make any difference? There are thousands of starfish on the shore."

The boy picked up another starfish, tossed it safely into the waters, and said, "It makes a difference to that one."

There are six billion people on this planet. God isn't asking you to reach them all by yourself. If each of us would do our small part to share God's love by our actions and words each day, it would make a difference. What individual can you help today?

COMMITMENT PRAYER

Father, I want to make a difference in other people's lives. Make my life count in helping others get to know You, in Jesus' name. Amen.

26

01 sun
02 mon
03 tue
04 wed
05 thu
06 fri
07 sat

He did not waver at the promise of God
through unbelief, but was strengthened
in faith, giving glory to God.

ROMANS 4:20

RECEIPT

I was walking out of the store with my new hockey stick in hand. The security officer at the door stopped me and told me I had to pay for the stick. I told him I had already paid for it. He didn't believe me. So I pulled out my receipt of purchase from my pocket and let him see it up close. Needless to say, I did not have to pay for that stick twice.

God has given us His promises as our receipts for all Christ has purchased for us in His death and resurrection. When the devil tries to make you pay twice, throw the promise of God's Word in his face and stand up for what's rightfully yours by faith!

COMMITMENT PRAYER

Father, I believe that all of Your promises are true. I will not allow anyone or anything to steal what You've already given me, in Jesus' name. Amen.

27

01 sun
02 mon
03 tue
04 wed
05 thu
06 fri
07 sat

I can do all things through Christ who strengthens me.

PHILIPPIANS 4:13

OPTIMISM

A young psychology student was once drafted to the United States Army to serve as a cook. He noticed that most of the soldiers turned down the apricots at the end of the chow line, so he decided to try an experiment.

The first day as the soldiers passed through the dinner line he said, "You don't want apricots, do you?" Ninety percent of them said no. The next day, he made an optimistic change, saying, "You do want some apricots, don't you?" This time half of the soldiers took them. The third day he said, "One dish of apricots or two?" Forty percent took two dishes and fifty percent took one!

What a big difference an attitude adjustment can make! Don't say, "You probably don't want to hang out with me this weekend, do you?" Instead, say something optimistic, such as "When should we go to that new restaurant? Friday or Saturday?" Communicate in a way that expects favor, and people will meet your expectations.

COMMITMENT PRAYER

Father, I choose to be an optimist. Let my words reflect a heart that is filled with faith, in Jesus' name. Amen.

28

01 sun
02 mon
03 tue
04 wed
05 thu
06 fri
07 sat

And I have filled him with the Spirit of God, in wisdom, in understanding, in knowledge, and in all manner of workmanship.

EXODUS 31:3

SOLUTIONS

One time during the 1904 St. Louis Exposition, a native of Frankfurt was selling his delicious dachshund sausages. Gloves were customarily given to the customers to wear while eating the frankfurters, but this vendor ran out of them. People didn't want to eat frankfurters by hand because they would get greasy. He tried unsuccessfully to get more gloves, but rather than quitting he developed a creative solution to his problem. He approached a local baker and had him make bread rolls to hold the frankfurters while people ate them. It worked extremely well, and hot dog buns were born.

When you encounter obstacles that traditional answers don't overcome, create solutions. Then nothing can stand in the way of your success.

COMMITMENT PRAYER

Father, You are the Creator, and You live inside me by Your Spirit. Thank You that I have Your creative potential, in Jesus' name. Amen.

29

01 sun
02 mon
03 tue
04 wed
05 thu
06 fri
07 sat

A false witness will not go unpunished,
and he who speaks lies shall perish.

PROVERBS 19:9

GOSSIP

A man gossiped about his friend. Soon his friend confronted him, and the gossiper became very sorrowful for the wrong he had done. He asked for his friend's forgiveness, which he granted, and asked if he could do anything to make things right between them. The friend said, "Take two down pillows and go to the center of town; cut the pillows open and wave them in the air till the feathers are all out. Then come back and see me."

The man did just as he'd been told and came back to his friend. The friend said, "I've forgiven you. But to realize how much harm your gossiping has caused me, go back to the center of town and collect all the feathers." The man regretfully realized it would be impossible to find and collect every feather.

Gossip hurts people, destroys relationships, and harms the gossiper. Gossiping causes people to distrust you. They are thinking in the back of their minds, *If they gossip about this person behind his back, what are they saying about me behind mine?* Respect yourself and others: Don't gossip.

COMMITMENT PRAYER

Heavenly Father, help me to not gossip about others. I choose to make friends by showing myself to be friendly, both to their faces and behind their backs, in Jesus' name. Amen.

30

01 sun
02 mon
03 tue
04 wed
05 thu
06 fri
07 sat

And whatever you do, do it heartily,
as to the Lord and not to men.

COLOSSIANS 3:23

EXTRAORDINARY

One time a reporter asked baseball legend George Brett what he wanted to do at his last career at-bat. Most people would have said they wanted to do what Ted Williams did in the same situation: hit a 400-foot home run. But George said, "I want to hit a routine grounder to second base, run all-out to first base, then get thrown out by half a step. I want to leave an example to the young guys that that's how you play the game: all out."

We must do the same in life. Everything you do, put all of your heart into it. Do it as unto God, because He will reward you. The difference between ordinary and extraordinary is simply the little bit extra. Go all out. Be extraordinary.

COMMITMENT PRAYER

Father, I will put my whole heart into everything I do, as unto You. I will go all out to pursue Your best for my life, in Jesus' name. Amen.

31

01 sun
02 mon
03 tue
04 wed
05 thu
06 fri
07 sat

Now the purpose of the commandment is love from a pure heart, from a good conscience, and from sincere faith.

1 TIMOTHY 1:5

ELVIS

"Elvis is alive," said an Elvis imitator standing outside Graceland, the late Elvis' home. This impersonator looked the part, had the right moves, and even sounded like Elvis ("Thank you very much"). But he was still outside Graceland. He had no access to all that Elvis had owned.

Our faith in God is to be sincere, real, and genuine. It's not just about going to church and looking the part of a Christian. If our faith is not real, we will live outside of God's kingdom's benefits. Let's not play the part: Let's live the life!

COMMITMENT PRAYER

Father, I love You with my whole heart. My faith is real, and my conscience is clear. Thank You for hearing my prayers today, in Jesus' name. Amen.

32

01 sun
02 mon
03 tue
04 wed
05 thu
06 fri
07 sat

And He said to them, "Take heed and beware of covetousness, for one's life does not consist in the abundance of the things he possesses."

LUKE 12:15

HAPPINESS

At the turn of the Twentieth Century, John D. Rockefeller was worth over $900 million. At that time he was still working hard and was making over $1 million per week. A reporter once asked him, "Mr. Rockefeller, how much money will be enough?" His response was "Just a little bit more."

God created each of us for a purpose, and that is to have a personal relationship with Him. When we aren't fulfilling our purpose we will have empty spots inside that nothing else can fill. Only by accepting Jesus as our Lord and Savior and developing a daily relationship with Him can we find the true meaning of happiness.

We can still have great things, but now we are able to *enjoy* those things because God has filled our empty spots.

COMMITMENT PRAYER

Heavenly Father, thank You that Jesus came to this earth to take the punishment that my sins deserved. Forgive me for my sins. I accept Jesus as my Lord and Savior and receive by faith Your free gift of eternal life. I ask You to fill the void in my heart with Your presence and Your love, in Jesus' name. Amen.

33

01 sun
02 mon
03 tue
04 wed
05 thu
06 fri
07 sat

For the wages of sin is death, but the gift of God is eternal life in Christ Jesus our Lord.

ROMANS 6:23

RESPECT

One night a young man, trying to steal gas from a parked motor home, placed his siphoning hose into what he thought was the motor home's gas tank. Then he sucked on the end of the hose to get the flow of gas started. He was rudely awakened when he realized his hose wasn't in the gas tank but the septic tank! When police arrived on the scene to arrest him, they found him curled up on the ground, sick to his stomach. I'm sure his self-esteem was knocked down to the ground right then, too.

After we sin we feel guilt and shame. When people lose all self-respect they can spiral downward into even more destructive habits and actions. Sin isn't worth the brief pleasure it may bring, and it always catches up with you. Protect your self-esteem by steering clear of sin.

COMMITMENT PRAYER

Lord, help me to steer clear of sin. I will place Your Word in my heart so that I might not sin against You. Thank You that with every temptation You will make a way for me to stand up against it, victorious, in Jesus' name. Amen.

34

01 sun
02 mon
03 tue
04 wed
05 thu
06 fri
07 sat

For I know the thoughts that I think toward you, says the Lord, thoughts of peace and not of evil, to give you a future and a hope.

JEREMIAH 29:11

CRITICS

Listen to what some movie critics wrote about these then-newly released films.

In 1939 one critic from *The New Yorker* wrote about a new movie: "Displays no trace of imagination, good taste, or ingenuity.... It's a stinkaroo." The movie was *The Wizard of Oz.*

Another critic once wrote about a strange new sci-fi movie: "O dull, new world! It is all as exciting as last year's weather reports...all trite characters and paltry verbiage." The movie was the original *Star Wars* film.

Remember, the critics in life are usually wrong. It doesn't matter what they say; it only matters what God says. And He says nothing but good things about you.

COMMITMENT PRAYER

Father, open my ears to hear Your voice. Lead me in the steps to fulfilling all of my potential, in Jesus' name. Amen.

35

01 sun
02 mon
03 tue
04 wed
05 thu
06 fri
07 sat

For I am persuaded that neither death nor life,
nor angels nor principalities nor powers,
nor things present nor things to come, nor
height nor depth, nor any other created thing,
shall be able to separate us from the love
of God which is in Christ Jesus our Lord.

ROMANS 8:38,39

BOXER

In a boxing match years ago, a fighter was getting frustrated because his opponent was dodging his every punch. So he pulled back to swing with all his might, and once again his opponent dodged out of the way. But this time he had swung with such force that he couldn't stop; the momentum of his swing brought his hand all the way around and right back to his own face. He hit himself so hard that he literally knocked himself out! The official gave the ten count, and pronounced his opponent the winner.

God has fixed your fight. You can't be separated from God's love, and that includes His victory and blessings—as long as you follow His Word. Don't knock yourself out. Claim the victory Jesus already won for you!

COMMITMENT PRAYER

Father, thank You that Jesus defeated my enemy when He died on the cross for me. I choose to succeed by following after Your Word, in Jesus' name. Amen.

36

01 sun
02 mon
03 tue
04 wed
05 thu
06 fri
07 sat

Delight yourself also in the Lord, and He shall give you the desires of your heart.

PSALM 37:4

EDISON

World-renowned inventor Thomas Edison worked relentlessly in his workshop, often going without food or sleep. His wife thought it would be good for him to take a rest, so one day she said, "You need a vacation."

Edison asked, "Where will I go?"

She said, "Decide where you'd rather be than anywhere else on earth and go there."

Edison smiled and said, "I will go there tomorrow."

The next day he awoke early and did just as he said he would do. He went out to his laboratory and kept on with his experiments.

When you love what you do, you will have a reason to get out of bed in the morning. And you can look in the mirror and say to yourself, "I like who I am, and I love what I do." Where your passion is, God's gifting and anointing in your life will be.

COMMITMENT PRAYER

Father, thank You for creating me for a special purpose. I will use the gifts You have given me to pursue the desires You have placed in my heart, in Jesus' name. Amen.

37

01 sun
02 mon
03 tue
04 wed
05 thu
06 fri
07 sat

And if children, then heirs—heirs of God and joint heirs with Christ, if indeed we suffer with Him, that we may also be glorified together.

ROMANS 8:17

HEIRS

In 1949 a young San Francisco man, out of work and money, took a walk along the beach and noticed a bottle partly covered in the sand. He picked it up and was surprised to find a note sealed inside, saying, "To avoid any confusion, I leave my entire estate to the one who finds this bottle."

The man went to authorities to find out whether the note was real. To his amazement, it was. A very wealthy woman from Europe, had written her last will and testament, put it in the bottle, and tossed it into a river by her home. This young man was awarded her estate of $6 million and $80,000 per year thereafter for the rest of his life.

You have an inheritance bigger and better than this. When Jesus died on the cross and then rose from the dead, God's will and testament—the Old and New Testaments—went into full effect for you. Follow the plan God outlines in His Word and you can take advantage of an amazing inheritance.

COMMITMENT PRAYER

Heavenly Father, I open Your Word and find the promises You have left for me. I receive them by faith, in Jesus' name. Amen.

38

01 sun
02 mon
03 tue
04 wed
05 thu
06 fri
07 sat

Then the man said, "The woman whom You gave to be with me, she gave me of the tree, and I ate."

GENESIS 3:12

BLAME

A young man who had an extensive criminal record was arrested for grand larceny, which he committed while under the influence of alcohol. He was sentenced to twenty-three years in prison. While in prison he filed a lawsuit against himself, stating, "I partook of alcoholic beverages, and as a result I caused myself to violate my religious beliefs." Then he asked the state to pay him $5 million for his violating his own religious beliefs. The court threw out his case.

If you blow it, don't blame someone else. Be bold enough to claim responsibility for your actions. Then go to God, admit your sin, ask His forgiveness, and avoid repeating your mistake.

COMMITMENT PRAYER

Father, I choose to be courageous enough to own my faults and correct them. I repent and ask forgiveness for hurting You or others. In Jesus' name I pray. Amen.

39

01 sun
02 mon
03 tue
04 wed
05 thu
06 fri
07 sat

And we know that all things work together for good to those who love God, to those who are the called according to His purpose.

ROMANS 8:28

ADVANTAGE

A man was on his way to the airport to catch a plane but was delayed by a flat tire. He was upset that he missed his flight #592 on Valuejet. However, a little later his frustration turned to solemn gratefulness when he was informed that the flight he'd missed had crashed just shortly after takeoff.

God is never the author of things that hurt people; Satan is. Every attack of Satan will eventually backfire in his own face when you give your problems to God. You don't have to let the enemy, circumstances, or problems steal your joy. Rather than getting stressed out, learn to take those things to God and place them confidently in His hands. Then leave them in there so He can turn them around for your good.

COMMITMENT PROBLEM

Heavenly Father, when I face difficult problems that try to rob me of joy I will place them in Your hands. I am confident that You love me and are working to turn all things around for my good, in Jesus' name. Amen.

40

01 sun
02 mon
03 tue
04 wed
05 thu
06 fri
07 sat

But we have this treasure in earthen vessels, that the excellence of the power may be of God and not of us.

2 CORINTHIANS 4:7

TREASURE

A man shopping at a flea market found a picture frame he liked for only four dollars. Since he didn't care for the picture it held, he removed it when he got home. A small, folded piece of paper fell out, so he opened it carefully. To his surprise, it was an old copy of the Declaration of Independence.

Just hours after the founding fathers of this nation signed the original Declaration of Independence on July 4, 1776, they had a printer make copies for distribution. The one this man found in his frame turned out to be one of the few original copies that survived, and it was in very good condition. He put it up for auction, and it brought in $2.4 million.

Inside you are hidden treasures, gifts from God. Seek God, and ask Him to reveal the talents He has given you. Slowly they will come to the surface. When they do, use and develop them to the best of your ability and let God's grace do the rest.

COMMITMENT PRAYER

Lord, thank You for the talents and gifts You have placed within me. I don't know what all of them are, so I ask You to help me find them. I commit to use them for Your glory, in Jesus' name. Amen.

41

01 sun
02 mon
03 tue
04 wed
05 thu
06 fri
07 sat

Those who are wise shall shine like the brightness of the firmament, and those who turn many to righteousness like the stars forever and ever.

DANIEL 12:3

CONVICTION

The *Guinness Book of World Records* contains countless examples of crazy things people will do just to be "stars," even if only for a few minutes. One man grew a 7'10" mustache! One man stood on one foot for 12 hours, 12 minutes, and 12 seconds! A teenager in India ate two rose bushes in 90 minutes; another time he ate 625 chilies in 90 minutes!

The Bible teaches that those who lead others to righteousness will be like stars and their glory will shine forever and ever. Do what is right. Be an example for others to follow. Use your life and influence to lead others to God. You will win respect, and your reward will last forever.

COMMITMENT PRAYER

Lord, I choose not to compromise Your Word and my convictions to fit in with the crowd. Help me be a star that shines out in this dark world so people will see Your love and presence inside me, in Jesus' name. Amen.

42

01 sun
02 mon
03 tue
04 wed
05 thu
06 fri
07 sat

"His lord said to him, 'Well done, good and faithful servant; you have been faithful over a few things, I will make you ruler over many things. Enter into the joy of your lord.'"

MATTHEW 25:23

COMPETITION

Bill Gates is on pace to become the world's first trillionaire. To give you an idea of how much $1 trillion is, imagine that you have $225,000. If you lost 47 cents in the sofa, Bill would have to lose $2.1 million to feel the same effect on his net worth as you would. If you made a car payment of $239, Mr. Gates would have to make a payment of $1.06 billion to experience the equivalent.

If you had to be the richest man in the world to be a financial success, then you might have a challenging road ahead. But if success for you is doing the best you can with what you have, then you have all the potential to succeed. Don't measure yourself against others. Compete with yourself: Be better today than you were yesterday and better tomorrow than you are today.

COMMITMENT PRAYER

Lord, thank You for giving me great potential. Help me to use all of Your gifts in me to their fullest. I will do everything with all my heart as unto You, in Jesus' name. Amen.

43

01 sun
02 mon
03 tue
04 wed
05 thu
06 fri
07 sat

And let us not grow weary while
doing good, for in due season
we shall reap if we do not lose heart.

GALATIANS 6:9

PERSIST

Early in a certain man's career he went into a promising oil venture with some friends. However, he soon ran out of money, so he sold his interest of the company to his partners. Shortly thereafter, his partners hit a large oil gusher and overnight formed the successful oil company Citgo. Next he went into the clothing business, but that did even worse. Next he tried politics and found that was a successful fit for him.

Eventually he was elected president of the United States. You have probably heard of this man. His name was President Harry S. Truman.

In life you will undoubtedly have some setbacks, but they don't have to hold you back. Stay after your dream. Never let it die, and never let it go. There is no telling where persistence can take you.

COMMITMENT PRAYER

Heavenly Father, thank You that no matter how many setbacks I experience they can't keep me from success. I will keep moving forward toward Your dream for me, in Jesus' name. Amen.

44

01 sun
02 mon
03 tue
04 wed
05 thu
06 fri
07 sat

In all your ways acknowledge Him,
and He shall direct your paths.

PROVERBS 3:6

DIRECTIONS

A man in Sweden took his grandson on a fishing trip sixty-five miles from home. On the way back he got lost and drove into Norway and then into the Arctic Circle. He drove three straight days, only stopping for gas and never asking for directions. Finally he fell asleep at the wheel and crashed his car into the side of the road, where authorities later found him and his grandson, unharmed. They were hundreds of miles from home.

Every day millions of people live like this grandpa. They are too stubborn to ask for directions. God has said that if we will seek His guidance in all we do He will direct our steps in the right path. Don't spend your life wandering aimlessly. Seek God's direction, and avoid getting lost in life.

COMMITMENT PRAYER

Father, Your Word is a lamp unto my feet and a light unto my path. Thank You for continually leading me on the path of righteousness, in Jesus' name. Amen.

45

01 sun
02 mon
03 tue
04 wed
05 thu
06 fri
07 sat

So shall your poverty come like a prowler,
and your need like an armed man.

PROVERBS 24:34

WORK

In South America a thief broke into a glue factory on a Friday night to steal two cans of glue, which he was addicted to sniffing. He couldn't wait to get home, so he opened up a can right there, put his head in, took a deep whiff, and passed out! When he woke up the next morning he found himself glued to the factory floor and unable to get up. On Monday morning, the authorities found him in that same spot, still glued to the floor.

Some people think the way to get ahead in life is by taking shortcuts, but that's really the way to lose everything they have. Respect yourself enough to work hard and honestly for what you want. You will appreciate it more, and you will be able to keep your success.

COMMITMENT PRAYER

Lord, I will build my life on the integrity of Your Word. Through hard work and dependence on You, my life will be filled with good things, in Jesus' name. Amen.

46

01 sun
02 mon
03 tue
04 wed
05 thu
06 fri
07 sat

Be diligent to present yourself approved
to God, a worker who does not need to be
ashamed, rightly dividing the word of truth.

2 TIMOTHY 2:15

I.Q.

A janitor who got tired of pushing a broom to clean the floors invented the Hoover vacuum cleaner. A farmer who had to do the laundry one day for his sick wife realized what hard work it was and invented the mechanical washing machine. A housewife invented Q-tips. Orville and Wilbur Wright, young bicycle mechanics, invented the first manned flying aircraft.

You don't have to be brilliant to be successful in life. God can use you even if you aren't an Albert Einstein. By the way, Albert had trouble in mathematics early in life and his teacher once told his father that he wouldn't amount to much!

Study hard, do the best you can, and God will give you the rest of what you need to succeed.

COMMITMENT PRAYER

Father, thank You for the mind You have given me. Help me to study hard and use it to the best of its ability. Thank You for giving me a spirit of wisdom and revelation and for opening up the eyes of my understanding, in Jesus' name. Amen.

47

01 sun
02 mon
03 tue
04 wed
05 thu
06 fri
07 sat

Then the Lord answered me and said:
"Write the vision and make it plain on tablets,
that he may run who reads it."

HABAKKUK 2:2

VISION

A young lady who lived in Illinois went to look for a job in the next town. She got lost and ended up in Indiana, a bordering state. Rather than pulling out a roadmap, she kept trying to find her way home by intuition. Soon she ended up in Pennsylvania, several states from Illinois. Border police finally picked her up in Maine, halfway across the country from her home.

Many people would rather drive through life, using their feelings as directions, than head toward a set of clearly defined goals. Don't drive aimlessly through life. Define your goals, and they will keep you on the interstate toward success in life.

COMMITMENT PRAYER

Father, show me the goals I should set and the steps I should take to achieve them. Thank You that You are thinking big thoughts about me, in Jesus' name. Amen.

48

01 sun
02 mon
03 tue
04 wed
05 thu
06 fri
07 sat

But in a great house there are not only vessels of gold and silver, but also of wood and clay, some for honor and some for dishonor.

2 TIMOTHY 2:20

LUXURY

It takes over six months to build a Rolls Royce; then, before it can roll off the assembly line, someone listens to the engine for eight hours with a stethoscope trying to detect the slightest imperfection. On the other hand, it takes only thirteen hours to build a Toyota.

Some Christians, like Toyotas, are in a hurry to roll off the assembly line. They don't want to spend time in prayer and God's Word to develop themselves to be vessels of honor.

Then there are the Rolls Royce Christians. They spend time reading the Bible, praying, and allowing the Holy Spirit to search their lives for imperfections and to fix them. Don't be an average Christian. Live your life in such a way that when you roll by, heaven turns its head in awe and says you are beautiful and rare.

COMMITMENT PRAYER

Father, I will make Your standards for quality, integrity, and passion the center of everything I do. Let people see Christ in me and give You the honor and glory, in Jesus' name. Amen.

49

01 sun
02 mon
03 tue
04 wed
05 thu
06 fri
07 sat

That you do not become sluggish,
but imitate those who through faith
and patience inherit the promises.

HEBREWS 6:12

TOMORROW

A young boy named Michael was fishing with his family along the Gulf of Mexico. Rather than be content to fish with a single line he decided to assemble a rope that would have several fishhooks attached, enabling him to catch more fish in less time. Some members of his family mocked his creative idea and said he was wasting his time. By dinnertime he hadn't yet caught a fish. After dinner he went to check his line and found that he had more fish on his line than the rest of the family had caught all day. It seems Michael Dell, founder of Dell computers, had the last laugh.

Today you are forming habits for success or failure. Be careful not to develop the character trait of listening to critical people. Instead develop the habit of listening to God's dreams for you.

COMMITMENT PRAYER

Father, help me see any bad habits I am developing in my life. Give me the wisdom and strength to change them to new habits I should be developing, in Jesus' name. Amen.

50

01 sun
02 mon
03 tue
04 wed
05 thu
06 fri
07 sat

Then this Daniel distinguished himself above the governors and satraps, because an excellent spirit was in him; and the king gave thought to setting him over the whole realm.

DANIEL 6:3

PROMOTION

Belgium isn't a military world threat, and it probably never will be. Why do I say that? Well, look at just one example of their unthreateningly low standards. When a soldier is due for a promotion in rank he has to take a multiple-choice test. To ensure that he is adequately prepared to pass, he takes home the answers to the test to study. Then, to pass he must correctly answer only twenty out of the eighty-five questions.

We live in a world with low standards in so many areas. As Christians we must be careful that we live by the higher standard of God's Word. Only then will we find favor and promotion.

COMMITMENT PRAYER

Father, I choose to live by Your highest standards. Give me the courage not to bend under the world's pressure but to always stand firmly on Your Word, in Jesus' name. Amen.

51

01 sun
02 mon
03 tue
04 wed
05 thu
06 fri
07 sat

A brother offended is harder to win
than a strong city, and contentions
are like the bars of a castle.

PROVERBS 18:19

RELATE

Some male computer programmers said that every computer
should be referred to as "she" for the following reason: "Even your
smallest mistakes are stored in long-term memory for later
retrieval." Female programmers retaliated with the following reason
that every computer should be referred to as "he": "They have a lot
of data but are still clueless."

Arguing using cutting remarks like these will never solve a problem or get a person further in
life. Learn the art of solving disagreements peaceably rather than using force or cutting
remarks. Develop good people skills, and there is no limit to where you can go in life.

COMMITMENT PRAYER

Father, I will do unto others as I would have them do unto me. I will love my neighbor as myself.
Teach me to have Your sensitivity and kindness toward others, in Jesus' name. Amen.

52

01	sun
02	mon
03	tue
04	wed
05	thu
06	fri
07	sat

No temptation has overtaken you except such as is common to man; but God is faithful, who will not allow you to be tempted beyond what you are able, but with the temptation will also make the way of escape, that you may be able to bear it.

1 CORINTHIANS 10:13

OUT

In the early twentieth century, the world-famous escape artist Harry Houdini, performing for fans across the nation, successfully escaped hundreds of jails in just minutes. However, one time he was presented with a great challenge. Inside the jail cell, he pulled out a metal pick from behind his belt and began to pick the lock. He began to perspire as thirty minutes passed, then an hour. After two hours of trying to pick the lock he leaned up against the door, and it swung wide open. The door had never been locked!

The enemy wants to lead us to believe that there is no way of escape. But God always makes a way out of every temptation and trial we face. Jesus already defeated every problem for us. He unlocked the door. The exit may not seem apparent at first, but keep standing in faith and you will soon see the way out.

COMMITMENT PRAYER

Father, help me never lose sight of the victory that is mine in Christ Jesus. Thank You that right now I am more than a conqueror and I stand victorious over sin, in Jesus' name. Amen.

53

01 sun
02 mon
03 tue
04 wed
05 thu
06 fri
07 sat

But you, when you pray, go into your room,
and when you have shut your door, pray to
your Father who is in the secret place;
and your Father who sees in secret
will reward you openly.

MATTHEW 6:6

UNBELIEF

Dave Thomas once invited an acquaintance named Dean to invest in his small restaurant business. Dean passed on the offer. That small business grew to become the national fast-food chain Wendy's.

Later a man invited Dean to invest in his new restaurant that featured chicken as its main menu item. He passed. That restaurant grew into the national food chain known as KFC.

Later Ray Kroc invited Dean to invest in his small hamburger stand. Dean declined. Ray later turned his hamburger stand into the largest fast-food chain ever, McDonald's.

Then a man invited him to invest in his son's new computer business. Dean passed because he thought the name of the business sounded funny. It was Microsoft.

Don't pass the opportunities that God has to offer. Unbelief stops God's power from working on our behalf. Be a person of faith who believes and expects life to be good to you, because we serve a good God.

COMMITMENT PRAYER

Father, open my eyes to see the many opportunities You set before me. I build my faith by reading Your Word daily so that I can seize these opportunities when they come, in Jesus' name. Amen.

54

01 sun
02 mon
03 tue
04 wed
05 thu
06 fri
07 sat

I have fought the good fight, I have finished the race, I have kept the faith.

2 TIMOTHY 4:7

FINISH

The Brooklyn Bridge, which links Manhattan and Brooklyn, is one of the most famous bridges in the world. The engineers of the bridge were a father-son team. During the construction a terrible accident claimed the father's life and left his son paralyzed and unable to talk. However, against all odds, the son devised a plan that would enable the completion of the bridge. He would still supervise its construction by tapping out instructions with Morris Code on his wife's arm, and she would relay his messages. After thirteen years of this the bridge was completed.

Success doesn't come to those who start but to those who finish.

COMMITMENT PRAYER

Father, I will not only be a good starter of what You give me to do but a great finisher as well. Help me to find encouragement in Your Word when I get discouraged. In Jesus' name I pray. Amen.

55

01 sun
02 mon
03 tue
04 wed
05 thu
06 fri
07 sat

That the God of our Lord Jesus Christ,
the Father of glory, may give to you
the spirit of wisdom and revelation
in the knowledge of Him,

EPHESIANS 1:17

POSSIBILITIES

Most young people have played with Lego's during their childhood. Here is an interesting fact that most people never realize. There are twenty-four possible ways to connect two Lego's that have eight studs each. If you add just one more eight-studded Lego, you will now have 1,060 different connection possibilities. But if you have a total of six eight-studded Lego's you have 102,981,500 different connection possibilities.

It is amazing how a little increase can yield so much potential. Wisdom is just like that. The more you get, the more possibilities you have. Make gaining wisdom a priority in your life, and watch your possibilities multiply.

COMMITMENT PRAYER

Heavenly Father, I desire to gain Your wisdom, not the foolish wisdom of this world. Thank You that those who seek wisdom will find it, in Jesus' name. Amen.

56

01 sun
02 mon
03 tue
04 wed
05 thu
06 fri
07 sat

And God is able to make all grace abound toward you, that you, always having all sufficiency in all things, may have an abundance for every good work.

2 CORINTHIANS 9:8

GIVER

Many wealthy people have been notorious for being tightwads. President Franklin Roosevelt used to mooch dollar bills off his valet to drop in the collection plate at church. Oil tycoon J. Paul Getty once installed a payphone in his house to keep visitors from making long-distance calls on his home phone. John D. Rockefeller, who 100 years ago was worth almost $1 billion, once gave a groundskeeper a $5 Christmas bonus, which he later docked from his pay when the man took Christmas day off to be with his family.

Just because you have a lot of money doesn't mean you will be generous with it. If you aren't generous now, you won't be later. God said He will give to those who are givers. Let God use you to bless others, and you will be blessed as well.

COMMITMENT PRAYER

Heavenly Father, use me to be a channel to bless those in need. I believe that as I give what I can afford, no matter how much, You will bless it and cause abundance to overtake my life, in Jesus' name. Amen.

Make the Zero Pledge

Lord, I make this solemn pledge in the name of Jesus. Zero depression. When feelings of discouragement and inadequacy come, I will resist them immediately. I choose to believe what You have spoken over me. I am more than a conqueror through Jesus Christ who loves me. I am strong; I am bold; I am able with Your help and by Your grace.

Oneighty.Pray

This world is extremely competitive and full of obstacles in the path toward success. But God has given every Christian a unique advantage in the quest to win in life. This advantage is the access we have through prayer to the almighty God and His power.

However, we must know and follow the guidelines that make our prayers effective. There are reasons that some prayers are answered and others are not. The next thirty-one devotionals will help you to step into a new dimension that will bring God's best into your life. Go ahead. Turn the page, and let's get started.

//oneighty.pray

04

01

01 sun
02 mon
03 tue
04 wed
05 thu
06 fri
07 sat

But without faith it is impossible to please Him, for he who comes to God must believe that He is, and that He is a rewarder of those who diligently seek Him.

HEBREWS 11:6

VW BUG

A friend in Florida prayed and asked God for the money to fix up and paint his Volkswagen Bug.

A few weeks later, it was stolen. He prayed again and said, "Lord, I ask You to bring back my Bug, and I continue to thank You for the money to fix and paint it." For several months he stood strong in his faith without any sign of an answer.

Then there was a knock on his door. Two policemen escorted him to his recovered Volkswagen Bug. It had been completely repaired and painted by a gang of thieves who had been preparing to sell it and gotten caught!

One of the rules of prayer is faith. We must believe that God is not only powerful but willing and ready to use His power to assist us each day.

COMMITMENT PRAYER

Father, I believe that You are alive and want to reward me as I walk with You. I pray with confidence that You will answer me, in Jesus' name. Amen.

02

01 sun
02 mon
03 tue
04 wed
05 thu
06 fri
07 sat

That you do not become sluggish, but imitate those who through faith and patience inherit the promises.

HEBREWS 6:12

PATIENCE

Once when I was praying at eighteen years old, God spoke to me. He told me that I would have a ministry that incorporated music, drama, comedy, and preaching and that it would touch the nation.

It took eight long years of faith and patience for that vision to come to pass, but I never let go. I never stopped praying and thanking God for its fulfillment. Finally, we launched a national Christian television program called *Fire by Night* that not only fulfilled my vision but even exceeded it!

When you pray according to God's will, be patient with His timetable. In the meantime, remember to praise and thank Him by faith that you have what you've believed Him for.

COMMITMENT PRAYER

Heavenly Father, I thank You that when I pray, I have my answer by faith. While I patiently wait for the manifestation of my request, I will praise You that it's done, in Jesus' name. Amen.

03

01 sun
02 mon
03 tue
04 wed
05 thu
06 fri
07 sat

"And whenever you stand praying, if you have anything against anyone, forgive him, that your Father in heaven may also forgive you your trespasses."

MARK 11:25

FORGIVE

Years ago I was praying intensely about something I desired to see happen. Not only was this prayer not getting answered, but things were actually getting worse. As I sought God, He spoke.

I had been holding unforgiveness in my heart toward a person who had purposely lied about me, trying to destroy my reputation with a person I deeply respected. When I called this person, forgave him, and cleaned up my heart, things immediately began to change.

Here's a rule of prayer: Don't expect God to help and bless you while you have hatred toward another.

COMMITMENT PRAYER

Father, I forgive and release any person—stranger, acquaintance, friend, or family member—who has hurt me in any way. I refuse to allow unforgiveness to stop my prayers from being answered, in Jesus' name. Amen.

04

01 sun
02 mon
03 tue
04 wed
05 thu
06 fri
07 sat

Enter into His gates with thanksgiving, and into His courts with praise. Be thankful to Him, and bless His name.

PSALM 100:4

THANKS

I have three boys who are already teenagers. There is probably nothing that moves my heart more than when they go out of their way to tell me "thank you" for something I've done for them. When I see that they are sincerely grateful for things they already have, it provokes a desire in me to do all I can to fulfill a future request.

When you approach God in prayer with praise and thankfulness for the good things He's already done, you are in strong spiritual position to trust Him for the future. Thank Him daily for His blessings and protection.

COMMITMENT PRAYER

Father in heaven, I want to say "thank You." I praise You for Your love, protection, and provision, which are evident in my life every day, in Jesus' name. Amen.

05

01 sun
02 mon
03 tue
04 wed
05 thu
06 fri
07 sat

The sacrifice of the wicked is an abomination to the Lord, but the prayer of the upright is His delight.

PROVERBS 15:8

DELIGHT

Today people have an unhealthy mixture of religious talk and wickedness in their lives. For example, we see our politicians who ascend to the highest offices in the land go to church, offer prayers, and ask God to bless America, while helping to make it legal to abort babies in the last three months of a woman's pregnancy.

When people live wicked lives, their "sacrifices" of church attendance and prayers are an abomination in the nostrils of Almighty God. God does not hear their prayers, and one day they will suffer the reward of the wicked.

On the other hand, God absolutely delights when we approach Him with upright hearts, and He takes joy in hearing and answering us.

COMMITMENT PRAYER

Heavenly Father, I confess and repent of any and all sin in my life. Thank You for giving me an upright heart, in Jesus' name. Amen.

06

01 sun
02 mon
03 tue
04 wed
05 thu
06 fri
07 sat

Redeeming the time, because the days are evil.

EPHESIANS 5:16

TIME

"I don't have time to pray!"

How many times have you heard people say this? How many times have you said it?

Where does all our time go? Well, according to USA Today, in the average American's lifetime, he or she will spend:

- six months at stoplights,
- eight months opening junk mail,
- one year looking for misplaced objects,
- two years unsuccessfully returning phone calls,
- five years waiting in line, and
- six years eating.

The truth is, we all have time to pray, but we don't always make time. Redeem your time and make a commitment to put prayer in your daily schedule.

COMMITMENT PRAYER

Father, thank You for giving me wisdom to prioritize my daily events, making the time to talk to You and study Your Word. In Jesus' name, I pray. Amen.

07

01 sun
02 mon
03 tue
04 wed
05 thu
06 fri
07 sat

"Therefore I say to you, whatever things you ask when you pray, believe that you receive them, and you will have them."

MARK 11:24

CHANCE

I don't know how many times I've walked into convenience stores and watched people desperately hoping to make all their dreams come true by buying dozens of lottery tickets.

However, it is interesting to note that buying even fifty lotto tickets every week increases your chance of winning the jackpot to about once every 5000 years!

You'd do better to spend your time seeking after God. He's promised to give you the things you desire when you pray with believing faith. Trust in God, not in man, and all His dreams for you will come true.

COMMITMENT PRAYER

Father, my hopes and dreams are in You. I seek Your face daily and believe I receive the things I pray for, in Jesus' name. Amen.

08

01 sun
02 mon
03 tue
04 wed
05 thu
06 fri
07 sat

But someone will say, "You have faith, and I have works." Show me your faith without your works, and I will show you my faith by my works.

JAMES 2:18

RUN

Two children were walking to school and were afraid they would arrive late. One said, "Let's pray and ask God to help us not be late."

The other replied in a practical way: "I'm going to pray while I'm running. I believe God will help me run fast enough to not be late."

God will not do for us what He has enabled us to do for ourselves. But when we have done all we can do with our natural strength, His supernatural strength will make up the difference.

COMMITMENT PRAYER

Father, I commit to fulfill the responsibilities You've given me in life. I ask You to go beyond what I can do to fulfill Your will for me, in Jesus' name. Amen.

09

01 sun
02 mon
03 tue
04 wed
05 thu
06 fri
07 sat

I can do all things through Christ
who strengthens me.

PHILIPPIANS 4:13

CHARGE UP

I grew up in the cold north of Canada. Some days were so cold that the engine and battery in the car froze up, making it impossible to start. When that happened, we had to recruit another car with a strong battery and running engine. We attached cables from the running car to the battery on our "dead" car, gave it a few minutes to charge, and then started it up.

When you pray and meditate on God's Word, you're getting spiritual battery cables from heaven in your spirit. Take time today to charge up with God's strength.

COMMITMENT PRAYER

Heavenly Father, help me to not allow myself to get cold spiritually. I'm staying connected to You each day to keep my spiritual charge strong, in Jesus' name. Amen.

10

01 sun
02 mon
03 tue
04 wed
05 thu
06 fri
07 sat

These all continued with one accord
in prayer and supplication....

ACTS 1:14

ONE

A couple years ago, I challenged our students at Oneighty® to join millions of Christians around the world in "See You at the Pole." This is an annual, national youth prayer gathering at school flagpoles on the third Wednesday morning of September. The students pray for protection, laborers, and revival in their schools.

After praying, Oneighty® members went into their schools and invited their friends to come to church that night. That evening 1553 students came, and 238 came to Christ!

Unusual power comes when we pray in one accord. Pray with others who have like faith and common goals.

COMMITMENT PRAYER

Father, I ask You to surround me with friends with whom I can pray in one accord for the desires You've put in our hearts. In Jesus' name, I pray. Amen.

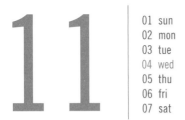

01 sun
02 mon
03 tue
04 wed
05 thu
06 fri
07 sat

For I am not ashamed of the gospel of Christ, for it is the power of God to salvation for everyone who believes, for the Jew first and also for the Greek.

ROMANS 1:16

POWER

I was sixteen years old, not saved yet, and had just pelted a muscle car with eggs. As I drove away in my very slow 1970 Duster, that hot, egged car was right on my tail. I pulled into a gravel alley, and soon the other driver stopped pursuing and backed up out of the alley. Why? He was afraid the rocks I was spitting up in front of him would chip his new paint.

Many Christians are just like that. They are filled with power because they have been born again, but they hesitate to go into a hurting, dirty world because they think it will mess them up. But that's what God's power is for! It's not there to show off in a church gathering but to take into a world that needs Jesus.

COMMITMENT PRAYER

Father, thank You for giving me power to proclaim the gospel with signs and wonders that follow. I will go to those who need to hear this Good News the most, in Jesus' name. Amen.

12

01 sun
02 mon
03 tue
04 wed
05 thu
06 fri
07 sat

Let us therefore come boldly to the throne of grace, that we may obtain mercy and find grace to help in time of need.

HEBREWS 4:16

HEAD OFFICE

A friend of mine who was involved in developing new cleaning products once took one of his new products to Wal-Mart's head offices to ask them to consider carrying the product in all of their stores. He told me that because so many people wanted to distribute products through Wal-Mart, they had to limit their appointment times and so had assigned him precisely fifteen minutes to make his presentation.

God is different. You can enter into His head office anytime, as long as you go in with great confidence. He is ready to give you grace and meet your needs.

COMMITMENT PRAYER

Father, I boldly come into Your throne room today. I accept Your mercy and forgiveness for my sins. I thank You for meeting all my needs, in Jesus' name. Amen.

13

01 sun
02 mon
03 tue
04 wed
05 thu
06 fri
07 sat

Remember now your Creator in the days of your youth, before the difficult days come, and the years draw near when you say, "I have no pleasure in them."

ECCLESIASTES 12:1

SHARPEN UP

A man in the woods was struggling to saw down a large tree. A friend watching noticed that he was not making much progress, so he said, "You really ought to sharpen your saw; it will cut better."

The man responded, "I don't have time to sharpen it. I've got to get this done."

The teenage years are busy with school, friends, movies, sports, and everything else you love to do. But you can't afford to block God out of your life and schedule. Build a strong spiritual foundation now. It will serve you well for the rest of your life.

COMMITMENT PRAYER

Father, I will not forget You in my youth. I believe that my time with You in the Word and prayer will empower my spirit daily to overcome every challenge, in Jesus' name. Amen.

14

01 sun
02 mon
03 tue
04 wed
05 thu
06 fri
07 sat

But seek first the kingdom of God and His righteousness, and all these things shall be added to you.

MATTHEW 6:33

SEEK

My heart nearly stopped. I had lost my wallet and the thousands of dollars in it. I was hours away from using that money as a down payment on our new home. Make no mistake about it: I didn't *look* for my wallet; I didn't just take a glance to see if I could find it. I furiously began to *seek* after it—and, thank God, I found it.

A looker is casual. A seeker is serious. When you get serious about seeking after God, you'll begin to see serious results and blessings in every area of your life. Don't be a spiritual looker. Be a seeker.

COMMITMENT PRAYER

Father, I commit to seek after You and Your kingdom. I know that when I do this, everything else in life will be added unto me, in Jesus' name. Amen.

15

01 sun
02 mon
03 tue
04 wed
05 thu
06 fri
07 sat

But if the Spirit of Him who raised Jesus from the dead dwells in you, He who raised Christ from the dead will also give life to your mortal bodies through His Spirit who dwells in you.

ROMANS 8:11

ALIVE

During the radical 1960s, many cultural leaders pronounced that God was dead. *Time* magazine's very first all-text cover boldly asked the question "Is God Dead?" John Lennon in his hit song "Imagine" encouraged listeners to imagine a world with no heaven, no hell, and no religion. Madeline Murray O'Hair gave national attention to the atheist movement.

More than thirty years later, "time" has certainly passed and things have certainly changed! John Lennon was murdered and discovered firsthand that there is a heaven and a hell. I recently met Ms. O'Hair's son, William, who is a committed, born-again Christian with a mission to send and distribute Bibles to Eastern Bloc nations.

God is alive and well! When we pray and see results, we become living proof that He is real!

COMMITMENT PRAYER

Father, I thank You for the resurrection life of Jesus that is at work in me to quicken and empower me today. In Jesus' name, I pray. Amen.

16

01 sun
02 mon
03 tue
04 wed
05 thu
06 fri
07 sat

Praying always with all prayer and supplication in the Spirit, being watchful to this end with all perseverance and supplication for all the saints.

EPHESIANS 6:18

OTHERS

Have you ever enjoyed a Wendy's hamburger? In his book *Well Done,* the late Dave Thomas, CEO of Wendy's International, wrote, "Many people who come to me, especially since my work on behalf of adoption started, say they're going to remember me in their prayers, and well, I take them seriously since I figure we all need as much help as we can get. I'm really thankful for people who pray for me."

God's Word encourages us to look beyond ourselves and pray for others. Who can you pray for today?

COMMITMENT PRAYER

Heavenly Father, guide my prayers today. I come to You on behalf of other people who need Your help. I believe my prayers will make a difference in others' lives, in Jesus' name. Amen.

17

01 sun
02 mon
03 tue
04 wed
05 thu
06 fri
07 sat

If you abide in Me, and My words abide in you, you will ask what you desire, and it shall be done for you.

JOHN 15:7

WESLEY

John Wesley, one of the great evangelists of his day, led thousands of people to Christ. What made his presentation of the gospel message so compelling and effective? I believe his success can be summed up in something he said and lived by: "God is limited by our prayer life. It seems He can do nothing for humanity unless we ask Him."

God has given you authority on this earth. As you pray according to His Word, you release Him to bring about your desires and to make changes where they are needed.

COMMITMENT PRAYER

Father, today I allow Your Word to live strong in me. And I live strong in You. Thank You for giving me the desires that I pray for in Jesus' name. Amen.

18

01 sun
02 mon
03 tue
04 wed
05 thu
06 fri
07 sat

Now this is the confidence that we have in Him, that if we ask anything according to His will, He hears us.

1 JOHN 5:14

THE WILL

Not long ago my wife, Cathy, and I discovered that she had been named as a beneficiary in her father's will. We were asked to attend the reading of the will and were given a written copy documenting all that her father had left to her.

No one can change what is in that will. It was the express will of her father, and it is the trustee's responsibility to carry it out.

You are in the greatest will ever written. It is the will of God as recorded in the Bible. He has given you promises that are sure. So read your will and trust God to bring it to pass in your life.

COMMITMENT PRAYER

Father, thank You for providing everything I need according to Your promises in Scripture. I receive Your express will for my life today, in Jesus' name. Amen.

19

01 sun
02 mon
03 tue
04 wed
05 thu
06 fri
07 sat

I desire therefore that the men pray everywhere, lifting up holy hands, without wrath and doubting.

1 TIMOTHY 2:8

NO DOUBT

The answer was a resounding "no!" The dean of the Tulsa, Oklahoma, Bible school that Cathy and I wanted to attend told us the school would not accept Canadian citizens. We lived in Calgary, Canada, about 2000 miles from Tulsa. Yet we felt sure that God had told us to go to this school.

So I graciously explained to the dean that we were coming anyway and pleaded with him to accept us. He told me we were wasting our time and money in coming. Three days of driving later, we stood in line to register at that school. We gave our names to the admissions director, and she smiled and handed us our student IDs.

We were in! I never found out why, except that when God decrees something, if we will respond with faith and not doubt, circumstances are subject to change.

COMMITMENT PRAYER

Heavenly Father, thank You that any negative circumstances facing me right now are subject to change. I lift my hands and voice today with faith in You, in Jesus' name. Amen.

20

01 sun
02 mon
03 tue
04 wed
05 thu
06 fri
07 sat

"And I will give you the keys of the kingdom...."

MATTHEW 16:19

KEYS

There I was outside my car looking in. The key was in the ignition, the car was running, and I was completely locked out! I was supposed to preach in fifteen minutes, and I had locked my keys in the car that was going to get me there. I felt so stupid, so helpless!

I learned a lesson that evening: Keep your hands on your keys. Keys are your entrance into the most important things in your world. Jesus gave us the keys of His kingdom. When we bind and loose things in prayer, we are exercising the use of our spiritual keys.

Pick up your keys today, and never allow them to leave your possession.

COMMITMENT PRAYER

Heavenly Father, I thank You for giving me the keys of power and authority in the earth. I will bind the works of darkness and loose the power of God in the world, in Jesus' name. Amen.

21

01 sun
02 mon
03 tue
04 wed
05 thu
06 fri
07 sat

Then He came to the disciples and found them asleep, and said to Peter, "What? Could you not watch with Me one hour?"

MATTHEW 26:40

ROCKY

Rocky rose out of obscurity to win the heavyweight championship of the world. Now he was on top—with fame, a big house, endorsements, and a wonderful wife. Then came *Rocky III!* He allowed himself to grow complacent and lost the "eye of the tiger." He stopped doing the things that had gotten him to the top in the first place.

The church is similar. We rose out of obscurity in our world on the Day of Pentecost about 2000 years ago. God has graced us with remarkable growth and influence. But in order to continue growing, we must remember what got us started: 120 disciples praying in the Upper Room! Let's return to the basics of praying and proclaiming His Word to this needy world.

COMMITMENT PRAYER

Father, I will not allow my heart to grow lukewarm or complacent. I stir up the gift of God in my life today, in Jesus' name. Amen.

22

01 sun
02 mon
03 tue
04 wed
05 thu
06 fri
07 sat

For I know the thoughts that I think toward you, says the Lord, thoughts of peace and not of evil, to give you a future and a hope.

JEREMIAH 29:11

TARGET

I'll never forget a Peanuts cartoon I heard about a few years ago. In the first frame, Charlie points his bow and arrow at a fence. The next frame shows the arrow flying through the air. In the final frame Charlie Brown paints a red bull's-eye around the arrow.

Each of us needs defined vision and direction. God wants you to have targets and goals that you are praying and shooting for. God has promised to show you a future that has peace and hope. Let Him reveal each step toward that future in prayer.

COMMITMENT PRAYER

Lord, thank You for helping me to stay on target with the future You've planned for me. In Jesus' name, I pray. Amen.

23

01 sun
02 mon
03 tue
04 wed
05 thu
06 fri
07 sat

But I will hope continually, and will praise You yet more and more.

PSALM 71:14

MORE

A few months ago I started lifting weights with the goals of toning up and increasing my strength. I remember trying to lift the same amount as was my training partner, who had been working out for several years. I couldn't even budge it! I was tempted to be discouraged, even to quit. Instead, I started with much less weight and stayed consistent, and I'm right on his heels now.

Our prayers, praise, and worship are the same way. We don't start out like spiritual Arnold Schwarzeneggers. Your time with God may start out at five minutes per day, but as you stay faithful each day, you'll see a desire emerge to increase more and more.

COMMITMENT PRAYER

Father, I take this time to praise You even more today than I did yesterday. You give me hope to live, in Jesus' name. Amen.

24

01 sun
02 mon
03 tue
04 wed
05 thu
06 fri
07 sat

He went a little farther and fell on His face, and prayed, saying, "O My Father, if it is possible, let this cup pass from Me; nevertheless, not as I will, but as You will."

MATTHEW 26:39

SPORTS

For different sports we have different rules. Can you imagine playing basketball with football's rules? Someone would quickly get hurt!

There are also different rules for different kinds of prayer. In this Scripture, Jesus offers a prayer of consecration.

"If it be Your will" is how we pray when we don't know the answer. However, we can't pray that kind of prayer when the will of God is already clear in His Word. It's already His will for you to be saved, healed, blessed, and forgiven. In those areas, offer the prayer of faith. Don't mix the rules of prayer.

COMMITMENT PRAYER

Father, I thank You for Your Word, which guides my prayer life. Your Word is a lamp to my feet and a light to my path, in Jesus' name. Amen.

25

01 sun
02 mon
03 tue
04 wed
05 thu
06 fri
07 sat

And the prayer of faith will save the sick, and the Lord will raise him up. And if he has committed sins, he will be forgiven.

JAMES 5:15

HEALTH

I had come home from a mission trip to Africa. Some kind of virus had gotten into my system, and my body was weaker than it has ever been. I lay in bed for two weeks and didn't get better, but worse. I went to several doctors, including "specialists," who could not diagnose this sickness.

Reality set in. This was a fight for my life. I went to the Word of God and followed its instruction. I called the elders of our church. They came, anointed me with oil, and prayed the prayer of faith. One day later I was on my feet, and two days later I was strong and back to work.

The prayer of faith is powerful! Thank God for doctors, but when they don't have all the answers, there is One who does!

COMMITMENT PRAYER

Lord, I thank You for Your healing power in my body. I walk daily in Your health and strength, in Jesus' name. Amen.

26

01 sun
02 mon
03 tue
04 wed
05 thu
06 fri
07 sat

Let the word of Christ dwell in you richly in all wisdom, teaching and admonishing one another in psalms and hymns and spiritual songs, singing with grace in your hearts to the Lord.

COLOSSIANS 3:16

RADIO

I was scanning my radio dial the other day. Moments later I found myself singing every word of "Hotel California" by The Eagles. It had been more than twenty years since, as a teenager, I had memorized every lyric to this song.

Music is a powerful force. That's why God has instructed us to sing the Word of God in our praise and worship to Him. Music helps to further embed His truth in our hearts and enables us to bring it quickly to our remembrance. Make time each day to worship God with song.

COMMITMENT PRAYER

Father, I am bold to sing and praise Your name today. Let the Word of God take permanent residence in my heart and soul, in Jesus' name. Amen.

27

01 sun
02 mon
03 tue
04 wed
05 thu
06 fri
07 sat

Jesus Christ is the same yesterday, today, and forever.

HEBREWS 13:8

MIRACLE

I tried a trampoline maneuver that I'd never done before: a double front somersault with a half twist. When I was done, I found myself in the hospital with two bones in my arm shattered.

Three months later X rays showed that my arm had not even begun to heal. The doctor said they'd have to "reset" the arm and start over with a pin in the arm. Surgery was scheduled.

One day later, my youth pastor prayed for my arm and told me that God had healed it. It didn't feel much different, but I went back to the doctor for new X rays. It was completely healed! The doctor said new bone had formed around the breaks overnight. He described it as a "supernatural phenomenon." I testified to him about Jesus!

Jesus hasn't changed. As you read about His power displayed in His earthly ministry, remember He's the same today!

COMMITMENT PRAYER

Father, thank You that You still heal, still do miracles, still save the lost, and still answer prayer, in Jesus' name. Amen.

28

01 sun
02 mon
03 tue
04 wed
05 thu
06 fri
07 sat

"Therefore pray the Lord of the harvest to send out laborers into His harvest."

MATTHEW 9:38

LABORERS

I had absolutely no plans to be a youth minister. In fact, I had no plans to be in any kind of ministry. I didn't come from a long list of preachers. My dad is a businessman, and I planned to follow in his footsteps.

Something happened. The clear call of God came into my life to labor in the harvest field of ministry. Why? It was because someone was praying for workers, helpers in the work of God.

Whom will you pray into the work of God's kingdom? If we're going to complete our job, we must have every laborer fulfilling his or her assignment.

COMMITMENT PRAYER

Father, today I exercise my faith and pray that You would give my church and the kingdom of God every laborer we need to get our job done for You. In Jesus' name, I pray. Amen.

29

01 sun
02 mon
03 tue
04 wed
05 thu
06 fri
07 sat

Therefore by Him let us continually offer the sacrifice of praise to God, that is, the fruit of our lips, giving thanks to His name.

HEBREWS 13:15

SACRIFICE

The sacrifices of the Old Testament were animals offered on an altar of worship to God. Each animal offered had to be spotless and unblemished and cost the worshipper something.

We offer New Testament sacrifices with our own lives and with praise from our mouths. We must be willing to lay our own lives down on the altar of commitment and offer the Lord praise with our mouths, even when we don't feel like it.

COMMITMENT PRAYER

Father, I bring You the sacrifice of praise today. I give You thanks for all You've done and are yet to do in my life, in Jesus' name. Amen.

30

01 sun
02 mon
03 tue
04 wed
05 thu
06 fri
07 sat

But you, beloved, building yourselves up on
your most holy faith, praying in the Holy Spirit.

JUDE 1:20

FOOD

Two dogs are in a fight. One is brown; the other is white. They are the same weight. They have the same disposition. They fight to the end.

Which will win?

The one you feed the most.

Your flesh and your spirit are at war with each other every day. Whichever one you feed the most is going to win.

The flesh is fed with ungodly entertainment, gossip, lust, greed, and all other acts of sin. The spirit is fed by worship, praise, prayer, Scripture, attending church, and all other acts of righteousness.

Feed your spirit, and starve your flesh to death.

COMMITMENT PRAYER

Heavenly Father, I build myself up today by praying and speaking the Word of God. Help me to avoid those things that feed my flesh, in Jesus' name. Amen.

31

01 sun
02 mon
03 tue
04 wed
05 thu
06 fri
07 sat

Do not love sleep, lest you come to poverty;
Open your eyes, and you will be satisfied
with bread.

PROVERBS 20:13

SLEEP

A man visiting his doctor described his condition in this way: "Doc, I sleep really well all night and all morning, but I'm tossing and turning all afternoon."

I have three teenagers who love to sleep. Most teenagers enjoy this recreational activity. In fact, I rather enjoy it myself. But, like anything else, sleep must be something we enjoy in moderation. Too much sleep will result in habits of laziness and steal precious time that God wants to use in our lives for fruitful spiritual activity.

So wake up, and make every day you have count.

COMMITMENT PRAYER

Lord, thank You for Your ability in me to discipline my mind and body to glorify You. I will not allow my life to come to spiritual poverty. In Jesus' name, I pray. Amen.

32

01 sun
02 mon
03 tue
04 wed
05 thu
06 fri
07 sat

The effective, fervent prayer of
a righteous man avails much.

JAMES 5:16

EFFECTIVE

Recently a man in a Munich, Germany, court tried to explain his motor accident to a judge by blaming it on God. This was his absurd explanation: "I let go of the steering wheel and asked, 'God, can You drive?'"

This was an ineffective prayer.

For our prayers to work and produce results, we must pray according to the guidelines found in God's Word. The Bible says that you should not tempt the Lord your God. When praying for a specific thing, make sure you have scriptural backup for your request.

COMMITMENT PRAYER

Father, help me to pray effectively by following the instruction of Your Word. Because of the power of Your Word, I know my prayers will accomplish much, in Jesus' name. Amen.

33

01 sun
02 mon
03 tue
04 wed
05 thu
06 fri
07 sat

Delight yourself also in the Lord, and He shall give you the desires of your heart.

PSALM 37:4

DESIRE

A lady once approached world-famous evangelist D.L. Moody on the street. She told him, "I'd like to get saved, but I don't want to give up dancing."

Though D.L. Moody preached against worldly dancing, he told her to come to his crusade, allow Christ to save her, and dance all she wanted to!

A few days later the same lady saw Mr. Moody again, ran up to him and exclaimed, "Now I know what you meant. I got saved two nights ago and now the 'want to' is gone."

When you truly give your heart completely to Christ, He'll replace your old, ungodly desires with His desires. And then He'll grant those desires as you trust Him in faith.

COMMITMENT PRAYER

Father in heaven, thank You for giving me Your desires and wants. I determine to delight in You. I believe that You are giving me the desires You put in my heart, in Jesus' name. Amen.

34

01 sun
02 mon
03 tue
04 wed
05 thu
06 fri
07 sat

"So I say to you, ask, and it will be given to you; seek, and you will find; knock, and it will be opened to you."

LUKE 11:9

ASK

In a recent survey people revealed what they would ask God (or a supreme being) if they could get a direct and immediate answer. According to this survey, 34 percent of the people said that they would ask, "What is my purpose here?" Other popular queries were "Will I have life after death?" (19 percent) and "Why do bad things happen?" (16 percent).

If only these people knew that God does provide direct and immediate answers when we pray and study His Word!

Go to the Lord with your questions and your needs. He's promised to answer.

COMMITMENT PRAYER

Father, I come today asking, seeking, and knocking. I believe that You give to me, help me to find what I'm looking for, and open every door I need to walk through, in Jesus' name. Amen.

35

01 sun
02 mon
03 tue
04 wed
05 thu
06 fri
07 sat

"Write the vision and make it plain on tablets,
that he may run who reads it."

HABAKKUK 2:2

VISION

When Habakkuk was praying, God spoke to him and told him to record clearly the vision and plans for his future.

In a recent study of alumni 10 years after graduating from a major university, researchers found that 83 percent had no goals. Fourteen percent, who had unwritten goals, were making 3 times as much money as their fellow grads who had no goals. The last 3 percent, who had written down their goals, made 10 times more money annually than the 83 percent who had no goals.

As you pray, write down the goals and vision God gives you for your future. Then pursue them with all your strength.

COMMITMENT PRAYER

Father, thank You for clearly directing my focus to the goals and vision You have for my life. Give me the strength and might to do my part to see them come to pass, in Jesus' name. Amen.

36

01 sun
02 mon
03 tue
04 wed
05 thu
06 fri
07 sat

Be anxious for nothing, but in everything by prayer and supplication, with thanksgiving, let your requests be made known to God.

PHILIPPIANS 4:6

WORRY

According to a recent study, today's young people have real worries. Of the teenagers studied, 53 percent worry about not getting into college, 52 percent worry about not getting good jobs, and 49 percent worry about dying.

What does worrying about something really do? Nothing. In fact, it can actually paralyze your ability to go forward toward success. When worry attacks your mind, fight back and overcome it with prayer, asking God for supernatural intervention.

COMMITMENT PRAYER

Heavenly Father, I refuse to allow my mind to be filled with worry and stress. I come to You with thanksgiving and boldly let You know my requests, in Jesus' name. Amen.

37

01 sun
02 mon
03 tue
04 wed
05 thu
06 fri
07 sat

What then shall we say to these things?
If God is for us, who can be against us?

ROMANS 8:31

Well-known PGA professional Greg Norman teed off and hit a long drive down the middle of the fairway. A gallery member shouted loudly, "You're the man." Norman's golf partner stepped up to the tee box and hit a drive sharply to the right and into a thick row of trees. The gallery member again shouted loudly but this time said, "You're with the man!"

Here's your good news today: *You're with the man!* God and His Son, Jesus Christ, are on your side and have all of heaven backing you. When you pray, you're putting God on your side and nothing can stand against you.

COMMITMENT PRAYER

Father, I thank You that no matter what I face today, You are bigger. I know that You are for me and nothing can stand against me, in Jesus' name. Amen.

38

01 sun	
02 mon	
03 tue	
04 wed	
05 thu	
06 fri	
07 sat	

But those who wait on the Lord shall renew their strength; they shall mount up with wings like eagles, they shall run and not be weary, they shall walk and not faint.

ISAIAH 40:31

EAGLES

Thank God He didn't say we would mount up like hummingbirds, woodpeckers, or chickens, but He said we would mount up like *eagles.* The eagle, our national bird, is a magnificent bird. It is more powerful than all other birds. It swoops down on its prey at speeds of up to 150 miles per hour and is able to carry twice its own weight. Its acute eyesight enables it to see something as small as a rabbit from as far as two miles away. The eagle lives in a high place in a nest that weighs more than one ton and can withstand winds of 100 miles per hour.

This is the kind of strength and power God will give you when you take time to wait on Him in prayer. People who pray mount up like eagles to soar to new heights. People who don't pray fall down. Pray!

COMMITMENT PRAYER

Father, today I wait upon You. I thank You for giving me the strength to mount up with the power of the eagle, in Jesus' name. Amen.

39

01 sun
02 mon
03 tue
04 wed
05 thu
06 fri
07 sat

He who dwells in the secret place of the Most High Shall abide under the shadow of the Almighty.

PSALM 91:1

On March 30, 1981, at the Washington D.C. Hilton, John W. Hinkley attempted to assassinate President Ronald Reagan. A Secret Service agent jumped between the sniper and the president, took the potentially deadly bullet, and saved the president's life.

If you dwell in God's secret place of fellowship with Christ through prayer, you have your own full-time body guard. God has promised to cover and protect you from physical harm. So the next time fear attacks your mind, pray and praise God for His constant protection.

COMMITMENT PRAYER

Heavenly Father, I'm dwelling in Your secret place of prayer and fellowship. I thank You for Your deliverance from every attack of the enemy, in Jesus' name. Amen.

40

01 sun
02 mon
03 tue
04 wed
05 thu
06 fri
07 sat

And when He had sent the multitudes away, He went up on the mountain by Himself to pray. Now when evening came, He was alone there.

MATTHEW 14:23

RETREAT

People's productivity increases when they receive appropriate rest. One study in Britain found that the productivity of workers who put in sixty hours a week decreased by 25 percent. They would accomplish more in
45 hours at 100 percent productivity.

This is one reason that God gave us the Sabbath. Even Jesus took time to retreat from His ministry, to pray, and to be refreshed. When we take time each week to rest from work and to attend church, where we pray and worship God, we are revived and revitalized.

COMMITMENT PRAYER

Father, I will keep the Sabbath holy and set it apart for rest and prayer. I receive Your refreshing, and I will accomplish the tasks You've given me, in Jesus' name. Amen.

41

01 sun
02 mon
03 tue
04 wed
05 thu
06 fri
07 sat

"Call to Me, and I will answer you,
and show you great and mighty things,
which you do not know."

JEREMIAH 33:3

HISTORY

World War II hero Winston Churchill helped lead much of the world against the forces of evil and Adolf Hitler. Churchill, who is well known for his powerful words, is quoted as saying, "History will be kind to me, for I intend to write it."

You can write the victorious history of your life and then live it out when you follow the Lord closely. He has promised that when you pray and call upon Him He will show you things to come in your life. He'll uncover your future and show you the steps in the right direction.

COMMITMENT PRAYER

Father in heaven, I believe that You can lead and guide each part of my life. Show me things to come in my relationships, my career, and my service for You, in Jesus' name. Amen.

42

01 sun
02 mon
03 tue
04 wed
05 thu
06 fri
07 sat

Jesus said to him, "If you can believe,
all things are possible to him who believes."

MARK 9:23

IMPOSSIBLE

Walt Disney was a visionary who believed he could do anything. According to one of his board members, Disney occasionally presented some unbelievable, extensive dream his mind was entertaining. Almost without exception, the members of the board would gulp, blink, and stare back in disbelief.

But unless *every* board member resisted the idea, Disney usually didn't pursue it. That's correct. The challenge wasn't big enough to merit his time unless they unanimously disagreed.

This type of faith is far too uncommon in the world and even in the church today. Let's trust God once again for the impossible!

COMMITMENT PRAYER

Father, thank You that nothing is impossible to me when I pray and believe. I choose to think big thoughts, dream big dreams, and do big deeds, in Jesus' name. Amen.

43

01 sun
02 mon
03 tue
04 wed
05 thu
06 fri
07 sat

"And it shall come to pass in the last days, says God, that I will pour out of My Spirit on all flesh; your sons and your daughters shall prophesy, your young men shall see visions, your old men shall dream dreams."

ACTS 2:17

MOVEMENT

USA Today recently reported a survey of 2000 teenagers who were asked to rate today's "in" activities. These were their varied answers:

- going to movies: 91 percent
- surfing the Net: 90 percent
- having a boyfriend/girlfriend : 86 percent
- partying: 86 percent
- sleeping late: 82 percent

Nothing was mentioned about serving God, but the Bible promises us that will change. Be part of a new movement that Acts 2:17 predicts will arise: a movement of young people who have a passion for God.

COMMITMENT PRAYER

Father, thank You for using me today to challenge the status quo and speak on your behalf. In Jesus' name I pray. Amen.

44

01 sun
02 mon
03 tue
04 wed
05 thu
06 fri
07 sat

And when they had prayed, the place where they were assembled together was shaken; and they were all filled with the Holy Spirit, and they spoke the word of God with boldness.

ACTS 4:31

TEAM

During the Chicago Bulls' string of world championships, Coach Phil Jackson emphasized teamwork. In years past, Michael tried but failed to win it all by himself. Jackson once inspired his team with a favorite passage by Rudyard Kipling:

Now this is the Law of the Jungle—as old and as true as the sky. And the wolf that shall keep it may prosper, but the wolf that shall break it must die. As the creeper that girdles the tree trunk, the law runneth forward and back. For the strength of the pack is the wolf, and the strength of the wolf is the pack.[5]

When we assemble, stand, and pray together as Christians, God increases His focus and power in us. Don't stand alone!

COMMITMENT PRAYER

Father, thank You for my brothers and sisters in the body of Christ. I believe our prayers will shake our school and impact our city, in Jesus' name. Amen.

45

01 sun
02 mon
03 tue
04 wed
05 thu
06 fri
07 sat

I will stand my watch and set myself
on the rampart, and watch to see
what He will say to me, and what
I will answer when I am corrected.

HABAKKUK 2:1

LISTEN

In Cambridge, England, a young man was so absorbed in the music on his headphones that he didn't hear a Cessna 150 crash-land on his lawn. Neither did he hear workers frantically rescuing its two injured passengers. He said the first moment he knew something was wrong was when he looked out his kitchen window and saw fire engines and police cars on his lawn.

Prayer is not just talking *to* God and getting results. It is also getting in a place that is quiet enough to listen to Him. So take time each day to turn off the stereo and the TV, unplug the phone, and fellowship with your Creator.

COMMITMENT PRAYER

Father, thank You that it's Your desire to speak to me. I set myself apart to receive Your wisdom and instruction today, in Jesus' name. Amen.

46

01 sun
02 mon
03 tue
04 wed
05 thu
06 fri
07 sat

[Prayers, intercessions] for kings and all who are in authority, that we may lead a quiet and peaceable life in all godliness and reverence.

1 TIMOTHY 2:2

KINGS

Would you like to be president of the United States for a week? If so, according to a recent poll, you are in the minority. The poll found that 52 percent of those surveyed would rather spend a week in jail than be president.

There is no doubt that our nation's leaders carry a heavy weight of responsibility in guiding our nation. It is important that we pray and intercede for both our local and national government leaders. We need to ask God to give our leaders wisdom and to help them make decisions based on righteousness.

COMMITMENT PRAYER

Father, today I pray for our president, as well as our local and national government leaders. Give each of them godly council, wisdom, and righteousness in all their decisions, in Jesus' name. Amen.

47

01 sun
02 mon
03 tue
04 wed
05 thu
06 fri
07 sat

And do not be drunk with wine, in which is dissipation; but be filled with the Spirit.

EPHESIANS 5:18

CRASH

In 1995, an Aeroflot chartered plane crashed near Baku, the capital of Azerbaijan. An inspector at the crash site said the crew had apparently forgotten to refuel the plane at its previous stop.

Many Christians suffer devastating spiritual crashes because they fail to refuel. God's two spiritual fuels for your spirit are His Word and communion with you in your times of prayer. Don't allow yourself to dip below "empty." Stay filled with the Spirit.

COMMITMENT PRAYER

Father in heaven, I commit myself to stay filled with the Spirit of God by praying, praising, and speaking the Word of God today. In Jesus' name I pray. Amen.

48

01 sun
02 mon
03 tue
04 wed
05 thu
06 fri
07 sat

Now faith is the substance of things hoped for, the evidence of things not seen.

HEBREWS 11:1

THE KEY

A terrible drought in a Midwest farming community threatened to ruin the entire season's crops. In a last-ditch effort, a local pastor assembled the entire community at the church to pray. The crowd gathered as the pastor stood atop a tractor and said, "Brothers and sisters, we have come here today to pray and believe God for rain."

"Amen," shouted the crowd.

"Well," said the preacher, "do you have the faith needed?"

"Amen!" the crowd shouted, even more loudly.

"Okay, I believe you. But one thing troubles me." The farmers were silent as they waited for the preacher to finish. Finally he said, "Saints, if you really believe, where are your umbrellas?"

Our faith is the key to seeing our prayers answered. We don't pray and hope for the best. We pray and believe it is done!

COMMITMENT PRAYER

Father, I pray today with faith and confidence that You hear and answer me. Thank You for meeting my needs according to Your riches in glory, in Jesus' name. Amen.

49

01 sun
02 mon
03 tue
04 wed
05 thu
06 fri
07 sat

Now the Lord came and stood and called as at other times, "Samuel! Samuel!" And Samuel answered, "Speak, for Your servant hears."

1 SAMUEL 3:10

NOISE

A Cherokee man and his friend were visiting downtown New York. Suddenly the former stopped and said, "I hear a cricket."

His friend said, "You're crazy! It's noon. People are jammed on the sidewalks, cars are honking, taxis are speeding by, the city is full of noise, and you think you can hear a cricket?"

"I'm sure I do," said the Cherokee. He listened even more closely, walked to the corner, spotted a shrub in a cement planter, dug into the leaves, and pulled out a cricket. He said, "My friend, my ears are different than yours. It all depends what your ears have been tuned to hear."

We must tune our ears to be sensitive to the leading and witness of the Holy Spirit. Tune out your noisy world and listen to God and His Word.

COMMITMENT PRAYER

Father, thank You for giving me ears to hear what the Spirit of God is saying to the church. In Jesus' name I pray. Amen.

50

01 sun
02 mon
03 tue
04 wed
05 thu
06 fri
07 sat

"He who has an ear, let him hear
what the Spirit says to the churches."

REVELATION 2:29

HEAR

Do you enjoy a good cheeseburger? If so, you can thank James L. Kraft, founder of the great Kraft Food Corporation, for the cheese. Mr. Kraft made, delivered, and sold his own cheese in Chicago in an old wagon drawn by a horse called Daddy. But on a gloomy evening long ago he was failing in business and had only sixty-five dollars to his name. With the reigns hanging listlessly in his hands, Mr. Kraft asked his horse, "Daddy, what is wrong with us?"

The horse was quiet, but a still, small voice spoke to Mr. Kraft's heart, saying, *What is wrong with you and Daddy is that you are trying to do this work without God. If you will listen to Me and believe in Me, nothing shall be impossible unto you.*

Mr. Kraft listened to God and went forward with confidence to build a great company.

God wants to encourage you each day with His Word. Read it and pray it out in your prayers.

COMMITMENT PRAYER

Father, I have an ear to hear Your voice. I thank You for the written Word of God that guides my steps, in Jesus' name. Amen.

51

01 sun
02 mon
03 tue
04 wed
05 thu
06 fri
07 sat

"If My people who are called by My name will humble themselves, and pray and seek My face, and turn from their wicked ways, then I will hear from heaven, and will forgive their sin and heal their land."

2 CHRONICLES 7:14

HUMBLE

In 1859, America was in recession. Money was in short supply, the stock market was nearing rock bottom, and people's spirits were low. In the midst of this Mr. Lamphier, a Wall Street clerk who was a devout Christian, started an event called the Fulton Street Prayer Meeting in New York City.

He sent out notice of the first meeting, to be held at the noon hour, and set up twenty chairs. The first noon, no one came. But the clerk prayed anyway, alone.

By the end of the next week the room was full, and soon similar meetings began to spring up in Philadelphia, Washington, Chicago, and other cities across the nation. These meetings gave rise to a great revival in America, and prosperity followed.

Revival begins with simple men and women humbling themselves in serious prayer. Let it begin with you.

COMMITMENT PRAYER

Father, I bow my knees and my heart to You in prayer today. I ask You to bring healing to our nation, in Jesus' name. Amen.

52

01 sun
02 mon
03 tue
04 wed
05 thu
06 fri
07 sat

Therefore take up the whole armor of God, that you may be able to withstand in the evil day, and having done all, to stand.

EPHESIANS 6:13

ARMOR

In World War II, Britain and America had a radio detection finder called "Huff-Duff." It intercepted transmissions between German U-boats and gave antisubmarine forces time to concentrate their strength for the kill. Used from the fall of 1941, the device offered a margin for victory in Atlantic antisubmarine warfare. Unaware that it existed, German headquarters transmitted top-secret orders to their submarine commanders. Ignorant of how completely the Allies had breached their security, the commanders found themselves to be targets instead of marksmen.

God has given us an advantage over our enemy. When we stand strong, clothed in the armor of God, praying the Word of God, we will destroy works of darkness.

COMMITMENT PRAYER

Heavenly Father, I put on the entire armor of God. Today I resist the forces of darkness and stand strong for righteousness, in Jesus' name. Amen.

53

01 sun	
02 mon	Righteousness exalts a nation, but
03 tue	sin is a reproach to any people.
04 wed	
05 thu	PROVERBS 14:34
06 fri	
07 sat	

LINCOLN

On February 11, 1861, Abraham Lincoln's farewell address at Springfield, Illinois, was brief. It contained fewer than 200 words. However, in this powerful address is found the core reason for our nation's prosperity and strength: "Without the assistance of the Divine Being, I cannot succeed. With that assistance I cannot fail." Believing these humble words of their president, the people of this nation could not help but prosper.

If the next generation of leaders wants to see the prosperity of America endure, you would be wise to continue to seek the assistance of Almighty God.

Remember this today: You can't succeed without the Lord; and with Him, you cannot fail!

COMMITMENT PRAYER

Heavenly Father, I pray that the standards of righteousness would be raised up once again in our nation. Exalt us so that we can exalt Your kingdom, in Jesus' name. Amen.

54

01 sun
02 mon
03 tue
04 wed
05 thu
06 fri
07 sat

"For everyone to whom much is given, from him much will be required; and to whom much has been committed, of him they will ask the more."

LUKE 12:48

MUCH

Recently a millionaire was fined for speeding in Helsinki, Finland. Police reported that he was traveling only 15 miles per hour over the speed limit. But the amount of the fine was $71,499! Why so much? It's because in Finland, a traffic fine is linked to the offender's income. The higher his income, the higher his fine will be.

To whom much is given, much is required! God has given us the awesome power to use Jesus' name in prayer to change things in our world to agree with His will. Now we are required to use what we've been given.

COMMITMENT PRAYER

Father, I take very seriously my opportunity to approach Your throne for help. Thank You for the authority You've given me to change things through prayer in Jesus' name. Amen.

55

01 sun
02 mon
03 tue
04 wed
05 thu
06 fri
07 sat

My voice You shall hear in the morning,
O Lord; In the morning I will direct it
to You, And I will look up.

PSALM 5:3

VICTORY

In October 1982, the Wisconsin Badgers' college football team was losing badly to the Michigan State Spartans. All of a sudden, the quiet stadium burst into cheers and applause for no apparent reason. Seventy miles away, in baseball's World Series, the Milwaukee Brewers were beating the St. Louis Cardinals. Obviously, many of the Badgers fans had tuned in their transistor radios to another game.

We must tune our hearts and minds in to the Word of God. Some days you may feel as if you're losing; but when you tune your spiritual ear to God's Word about what God is doing in you, you will rejoice.

COMMITMENT PRAYER

Father, I turn my heart and mind to You and attentively acknowledge Your Word in my life. I lift my voice and declare that I am victorious through the blood of Jesus. In Jesus' name I pray. Amen.

56

01 sun
02 mon
03 tue
04 wed
05 thu
06 fri
07 sat

A man's heart plans his way,
but the Lord directs his steps.

PROVERBS 16:9

NIKE

He dropped out of college. He had a dream to put "swooshes" on the feet of America. His name is Phil Knight, founder of Nike. How did he get started? He began traveling to the athletic dorms at universities in Washington and Oregon. He would back up his car, open the trunk, and sell his shoes to college athletes. One step at a time, Phil Knight's shoes would eventually dominate the marketplace.

As you pray and develop your vision, learn to take one step at a time. You can't make $1000 until you've made $10. You can't become a company president until you've worked in the warehouse.

Let God speak to you and give you simple steps to take you up the ladder to success.

COMMITMENT PRAYER

Father, I believe that as I plan my way You direct my steps. Help me to beware of unwise leaps, in Jesus' name. Amen.

Make the Zero Pledge

Lord, right now I make this solemn pledge before You. Zero prayerless living. I will take time each day to talk to You. To worship You. I believe my prayers are heard and that answers are immediately on the way. Your Word gives me that confidence. In Jesus' name. Amen.

Endnotes

1 John Maxwell, *21 Irrefutable Laws of Leadership*, (Nashville: Thomas Nelson, 1998) p. 97.

2 A.E. Winship, Abridgement of *Jukes-Edwards*, R.L. Myers & Co., 1990.

3 Ibid.

4 Dave Thomas with Ron Beyma, *Well Done! The Common Guys Guide to Everyday Success* (Grand Rapids: Zondervan, 1994).

5 Rudyard Kipling, *The Law of the Jungle* from "The Jungle Book," <www.poetryloverspage.com/poets/kipling/kipling_ind.html>.

Prayer of Salvation

God loves you—no matter who you are, no matter what your past. God loves you so much that He gave His one and only begotten Son for you. The Bible tells us that "…whoever believes in him shall not perish but have eternal life" (John 3:16 NIV). Jesus laid down His life and rose again so that we could spend eternity with Him in heaven and experience His absolute best on earth. If you would like to receive Jesus into your life, say the following prayer out loud and mean it from your heart.

Heavenly Father, I come to You admitting that I am a sinner. Right now, I choose to turn away from sin, and I ask You to cleanse me of all unrighteousness. I believe that Your Son, Jesus, died on the cross to take away my sins. I also believe that He rose again from the dead so that I might be forgiven of my sins and made righteous through faith in Him. I call upon the name of Jesus Christ to be the Savior and Lord of my life. Jesus, I choose to follow You and ask that You fill me with the power of the Holy Spirit. I declare that right now I am a child of God. I am free from sin and full of the righteousness of God. I am saved in Jesus' name. Amen.

If you prayed this prayer to receive Jesus Christ as your Savior for the first time, please contact us on the Web at www.harrisonhouse.com to receive a free book.

Or you may write to us at

Harrison House

P.O. Box 35035

Tulsa, Oklahoma 74153

What Is Oneighty®?

Oneighty® began as a local church youth ministry founded by Pastor Willie George in the fall of 1995. Shortly thereafter, Pastor George invited Blaine Bartel to join him in directing the program. Oneighty® has quickly grown to be one of the largest local church youth ministries in the nation, attracting 2500 teenagers each week. The Oneighty® program continues to grow nationally as well, with over 400 affiliated youth ministry programs across North America.

To contact Oneighty®, write:

Oneighty®
P.O. Box 770
Tulsa, OK 74101
Or visit them on the web at:
www.Oneighty.com

Meet Blaine Bartel

Past: Came to Christ at age 16 on the heels of the Jesus movement. While in pursuit of a professional freestyle skiing career, answered God's call to reach young people. Developed and hosted groundbreaking television series *Fire by Nite.* Planted and pastored a growing church in Colorado Springs.

Present: Serves under his pastor and mentor of more than 20 years, Willie George, senior pastor of 12,000-member Church on the Move in Tulsa, Oklahoma. Youth pastor of Oneighty®, America's largest local church youth ministry, which reaches more than 2500 students weekly. National director of Oneighty's worldwide outreaches, including a network of over 400 affiliated youth ministries. Host of *Elevate,* one of the largest annual youth leadership training conferences in the nation. Host of *Thrive™*, youth leader audio resource series listened to by thousands each month.

Passion: Summed up in three simple words: "Serving America's Future." Life quest is "to relevantly introduce the person of Jesus Christ to each new generation of young people, leaving footprints for future leaders to follow."

Personal: Still madly in love with his wife and partner of 22 years, Cathy. Raising three boys who love God, Jeremy—18, Dillon—16, and Brock—14. Avid hockey player and fan, with a rather impressive Gretzky memorabilia collection.

To contact Blaine Bartel,
write:

Blaine Bartel
Serving America's Future
P.O. Box 691923
Tulsa, OK 74169

www.blainebartel.com

*Please include your prayer requests
and comments when you write.*

Other Books by Blaine Bartel

Ten Rules of Youth Ministry and
Why Oneighty® Breaks Them All

every teenager's
little black book
on sex and dating

every teenager's
little black book
on cool

every teenager's
little black book
on cash

every teenager's
little black book
of hard to find information

little black book
for graduates

Additional copies of this book
are available from your local bookstore.

If this book has been a blessing to you
or if you would like to see more of the Harrison House product line,
please visit us on our website at
www.harrisonhouse.com.

HARRISON HOUSE
Tulsa, Oklahoma

The Harrison House Vision

Proclaiming the truth and the power

Of the Gospel of Jesus Christ

With excellence;

Challenging Christians to

Live victoriously,

Grow spiritually,

Know God intimately.